AND THE BAN PLAYED ON: THE "PUBLIC SAFETY" THREAT TO INDIVUAL RIGHTS

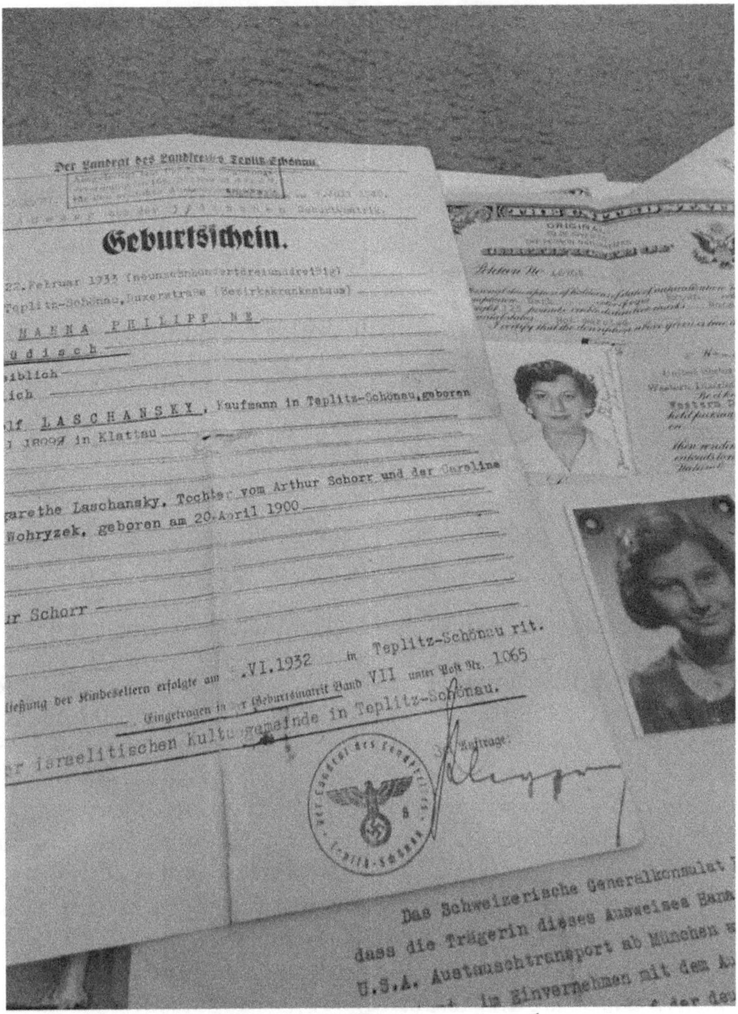

Marc A. Greendorfer[1]

---

[1] *Copyright © 2013 by Marc A. Greendorfer.

Contents

Life in a Post-Heller World 11
The District Court Orders 13
    The San Francisco Order 18
        Intermediate Scrutiny as Applied in the San Francisco Order 29
    The Sunnyvale Order 37
        The Sunnyvale Order under Intermediate Scrutiny 42
Precedent in Cases Involving Government Infringement of Constitutional and Other Rights 50
    Same Sex Marriage 50
    Speech and Assembly Restrictions under the First Amendment 63
        Abortion Clinic Protest Restrictions 64
        Gang Injunctions 68

Marc A. Greendorfer received his Bachelor of Arts degree from the University of California, Davis in 1986. He received his Juris Doctorate from Benjamin N. Cardozo School of Law in 1996. He graduated magna cum laude and served as Articles Editor-Submissions of the Cardozo Law Review from 1995 to 1996. After working at AmLaw 100 law firms in New York and San Francisco, Mr. Greendorfer founded Tri Valley Law in 2008, where he is currently a partner. Mr Greendorfer's other scholarly papers are available at http://ssrn.com/author=2133013. The image on the cover of this paper is of the author's mother's identification papers, issued by the Nazi occupation regime in her native Czechoslovakia during the Holocaust. This paper was inspired by the author's family's experience with being disarmed and persecuted by an omnipotent and abusive central government.

    Violent Video Game Restrictions 72

    Government Responses to the AIDS Epidemic 83

    Stop and Frisk" Police Practices under the Fourth Amendment. 93

Comparative Public Safety Data 100

The Nature of the Second Amendment Right Balanced Against Legitimate Government Interests. 133

    The District Court Orders compared to Morales 154

    The District Court Orders compared to *Brown* 162

        The District Court Orders compared to the SDNY Opinion 169

        The District Court Orders Compared to *Perry* 170

        The District Court Orders compared to *Hill* and *Schenck* 172

        The District Court Orders Compared to Government Responses to the AIDS Epidemic 173

Proposed Standard for Second Amendment Cases 203

Conclusion 214

In less than one month in early 2014, two Federal District Courts in the State of California[2] issued orders denying preliminary injunctions against two local ordinances that banned the possession of ammunition magazines that were theretofore otherwise legal to possess in California. Both courts admitted that a Second Amendment right was at stake but determined that, under intermediate scrutiny, the bans did not violate the Second Amendment, as the public safety concerns were sufficient to justify what the courts found to be a rather limited burden on Second Amendment rights.

---

[2] Throughout this paper the two orders are referred to as the "District Court Orders". They are San Francisco Veteran Police Officers Ass'n v. City & Cnty. of San Francisco, C-13-05351 WHA, 2014 WL 644395 (N.D. Cal. Feb. 19, 2014) (hereinafter the "San Francisco Order" and the court issuing the order being the "San Francisco Court") and Fyock v. City of Sunnyvale C-13-5807-RMW (N.D. CA. Mar. 5, 2014) (hereinafter the "Sunnyvale Order" and the court issuing the order being the "Sunnyvale Court").

The District Court Orders are quite troubling on a number of grounds and should be of concern to a wide variety of constituencies, particularly those with an interest in the exercise of rights that are generally seen as the province of minority groups.

Both courts facially relied upon the decision in District of Columbia v. Heller[3] as a starting point in their analysis, but in doing so they ignored one of the key points made in the *Heller* decision, and in so doing inverted the basic system of rights and protections that were established by this nation's founders and the framers of the Constitution.

Throughout the founding documents of this nation it is explicitly stated that individual rights come from the

---

[3] District of Columbia v. Heller, 554 U.S. 570 (2008).

sovereign creator of mankind, not from government.[4] The government was established by the people to further enable those rights and to provide a basic underpinning of a civil, commerce-driven society.[5]

Justice Scalia, in his *Heller* opinion, confirmed that the Second Amendment was a codification of an existing right, not the empowerment of government to grant, and withhold, such rights:

> … it has always been widely understood that the Second Amendment, like the First and Fourth

---

[4] THE DECLARATION OF INDEPENDENCE para. 2 (U.S. 1776) ("…all men are created equal, that they are endowed by their Creator with certain unalienable Rights, that among these are Life, Liberty and the pursuit of Happiness.--That to secure these rights, Governments are instituted among Men, deriving their just powers from the consent of the governed…)

[5] *Id.* at para. 6.

Amendments, codified a pre-existing right[6] …the historical reality that the Second Amendment was not intended to lay down a 'novel principl[e]' but rather codified a right 'inherited from our English ancestors'.[7]

The District Court Orders thus represent an upending of a founding presumption of this nation. Now, according to the District Courts, it is government that has omnipotent rights and individuals are only allowed those rights that the government grants.

The District Court orders reflect a common misunderstanding, or, perhaps, obfuscation, that the prefatory clause of the Second Amendment[8] represents the

---

[6] *Heller*, slip op. at 19.

[7] *Id.* at 26 (quoting Robertson v. Baldwin, 165 U. S. 275, 281 (1897))

[8] "A well regulated Militia, being necessary to the security of a free State, the right of the people to keep and bear Arms, shall not be

establishment of the individual right to keep and bear arms.

What the Second Amendment actually establishes is a limitation on the government's power to undermine organized groups of citizens from acting in the form of a militia. In other words, there are two rights involved. The first right is the fundamental right of individuals to own and use arms for their defense, subsistence, pleasure or anything else that they desire. This right is independent of government and inherent in every human being. The framers assumed that the Ninth Amendment, read in conjunction with the Second Amendment, would make this crystal clear.[9]

---

infringed." U.S. CONST. AMEND. II. The prefatory clause is the text prior to "...the right of the people...".

[9] *Heller*, slip op. at 5

> The first salient feature of the operative clause is that it codifies a "right of the people." The unamended constitution and the Bill of Rights use the phrase "right of the people" two

The second right involved is the right of individuals to organize in a militia to act in concert, bearing arms, to protect the state from governmental overreach. This is the *raison d'etre* of the prefatory clause to the Second Amendment —it is at once the affirmation and codification of the pre-existing individual right to keep and bear arms for whatever purpose the individual desires *and* a grant of rights for individuals to bear arms as part of an organized militia.

This affirmation was needed because, at the time of

---

other times, in the First Amendment's Assembly-and-Petition Clause and in the Fourth Amendment's Search-and-Seizure Clause. The Ninth Amendment uses very similar terminology ("The enumeration in the Constitution, of certain rights, shall not be construed to deny or disparage others retained by the people"). All three of these instances unambiguously refer to individual rights, not "collective" rights, or rights that may be exercised only through participation in some corporate body.

the ratification of the Constitution, the question of standing armies and the militia was still one of an evolving relationship. The Second Amendment was drafted to ensure that the federal government's rights respecting raising and maintaining armies wouldn't be used to strip groups of individuals acting as a militia of their natural rights to keep and bear arms. This limitation on government power respecting militias was in no way intended to be a grant of, or limitation on, the pre-existing individual right to keep and bear arms for all other purposes.

What can't be overlooked is the basic principle upon which the United States was founded: The government's rights are limited and enumerated; individual rights are otherwise unlimited and presumed to be sacred. As a corollary to this, the government, if it seeks to enact laws that restrict the rights of the people, has the burden of proving first that it has the authority to do so and second that there is a legitimate reason for the proposed restriction and that the scope of the proposed restriction is not overbroad.

With that as background, this paper will examine in detail the rationale for upholding the constitutionality of firearms restrictions since the *Heller* decision, focusing on the District Court Orders. Next, this paper will provide an overview of the scope of firearms restrictions currently in place and those being proposed, using California as the example of the most aggressive of such laws. Finally, this paper will extrapolate from the permissible firearms restrictions what would happen if the rationale used to uphold those laws were applied to restrict the exercise of other individual rights.

i) Life in a Post-Heller World

We start with the seminal case of *Heller*, where the United States Supreme Court found that the Second Amendment to the United States Constitution protects the pre-existing right of individuals to keep and bear firearms in their homes.[10] There is no shortage of commentary and analysis of *Heller*, and the purpose of this paper is not to argue for or against *Heller* but rather to analyze state and local lawmaking in a post-*Heller* world. Thus, for purposes of this paper, the critical element to take from *Heller* is that the United States Supreme Court, in finding an affirmation of the individual right to keep and bear arms, did not announce which standard of scrutiny applied to Second

---

[10] For an overview of the history and ramifications of *Heller*, see Eugene Volokh, *Implementing the Right to Keep and Bear Arms for Self-Defense: An Analytical Framework and a Research Agenda*, 56 U.C.L.A. L. REV. 1443, 1449-61 (2009) and Brannon P. Denning and Glenn H. Reynolds, Heller, *High Water(mark)? Lower Courts and the New Right to Keep and Bear Arms*, 60 HASTINGS L.J. 1245. *Heller* was subsequently applied to the states in McDonald v. Chicago, 561 U.S. 3025 (2010).

Amendment cases. The *Heller* opinion simply stated that whatever standard future courts applied to Second Amendment cases, it would have to be above the "rational basis" level.[11] Consequently any Second Amendment case has to be reviewed under nothing less than intermediate scrutiny.

In the absence of any further guidance from the United States Supreme Court, a number of lower federal courts have decided Second Amendment cases using an intermediate scrutiny standard. Among those are the District Court Orders.

ii) The District Court Orders

In late 2013, the California cities of San Francisco and Sunnyvale each enacted bans on firearms magazines

---

[11] *Heller*, slip op. at 56-57.

that had the capacity to hold more than 10 rounds of ammunition.[12] Each Magazine Ban is substantially similar to the other in wording and effect-they both require any person who had legally possessed[13] these so-called "large-capacity magazines"[14] prior to the effective date of the laws

---

[12] The San Francisco ban is codified at San Francisco Police Code § 619 (hereinafter, the "San Francisco Magazine Ban") and the Sunnyvale ban is codified at Sunnyvale Municipal Code § 9.44.030-60 (hereinafter, the "Sunnyvale Magazine Ban" and together with the San Francisco Magazine ban, the "Magazine Bans".)

[13] While the sale or manufacture of firearms magazines with capacities in excess of 10 rounds of ammunition has been prohibited in California since 1999 pursuant to Cal. Penal Code § 32310 (hereinafter, the "Statewide Ban"), the possession of such magazines in California generally is permitted for anyone who legally possessed those magazines prior to the effective date of the Statewide Ban

[14] Ammunition magazines with a capacity to hold more than 10 rounds are very common in the United States, as the Sunnyvale Order acknowledges, and are often referred to as "standard capacity magazines". Nonetheless, the District Court Orders and the Magazine Bans referred to standard capacity magazines by the politically charged term "large capacity magazine", that term will be used in quotes herein as a reminder that the term is not generally accepted as a description or phrase.

to either transfer the magazines out of the respective city in accordance with applicable law or surrender the magazines to the local police.

The purported impetus for the Magazine Bans was the 2012 massacre at Sandy Hook Elementary School in Newtown, Connecticut, where 26 people, including 20 young children, were killed by a mentally ill assailant who was obsessed with violent video games and mass murder incidents.[15] While there were many factors that led to the Sandy Hook massacre, from the failures of the mental health system to the lack of adequate security in the school

---

[15] *See* Colleen Curry, *Sandy Hook Report Offers Grim Details of Adam Lanza's Bedroom* ABC NEWS (Nov. 25, 2013), available at http://abcnews.go.com/US/sandy-hook-report-inside-gunman-adam-lanzas-bedroom/story?id=21009111 . *See, also, Sandy Hook Final Report*, OFFICE OF THE STATE'S ATTORNEY, JUDICIAL DISTRICT OF DANBURY. STEPHEN J. SEDENSKY III, STATE'S ATTORNEY (Nov. 25, 2013), available at http://www.ct.gov/csao/lib/csao/Sandy_Hook_Final_Report.pdf (hereinafter, the "Lanza Report"), where Adam Lanza was described as being "...afflicted with mental health problems". *Id.* at 29.

to the availability of detailed information that glorified mass murders to the effects of violent video games on the mental state of the assailant,[16] the cities of San Francisco and Sunnyvale ignored all factors other than the final step in the assailant's crime—the use of a weapon that had the ability to accept magazines with a capacity of more than 10 rounds of ammunition.

The Sunnyvale Magazine Ban was proposed to Sunnyvale voters as a ballot measure and it received a mere 12,404 votes in favor out of a total population of approximately 150,000.[17] The San Francisco Magazine

---

[16] *See* the Lanza Report, *supra* note 15 at 26-27, listing items found on Adam Lanza's computer, including videos of suicides, videos dramatizing the murder of children, computer simulations where the player controls a character that shoots children in a school and detailed spreadsheets on prior mass murder incidents and plans for replicating those massacres.

[17] *See* http://results.enr.clarityelections.com/CA/Santa_Clara/49877/123386/Web01/en/summary.html for Sunnyvale Measure C for voting results

Ban wasn't even presented to voters; rather, it was approved by 11 individuals, constituting the San Francisco Board of Supervisors, and signed by the mayor of San Francisco.[18]

Shortly after the Magazine Bans were enacted but before they would have required the surrender or transfer of the subject magazines, they were challenged by residents of each city, seeking preliminary injunctions, on the basis that each Magazine Ban violated the respective plaintiffs' Second Amendment rights.

---

and http://factfinder2.census.gov/faces/tableservices/jsf/pages/productview.xhtml?src=bkmk for population statistics.

[18] *See Unconstitutional Ban on Standard-Capacity Magazines Approved By San Francisco Board of Supervisors* November 1, 2013, available at http://www.nraila.org/legislation/state-legislation/2013/11/california-unconstitutional-ban-on-standard-capacity-magazines-approved-by-san-francisco-board-of-supervisors.aspx

Both challenges to the Magazine Bans were denied pursuant to the District Court Orders. Shortly after the Sunnyvale Order was issued, an emergency application for injunction was filed with the United States Supreme Court[19] and was denied without comment on March 12, 2014.[20]

(1) The San Francisco Order

In the case of the San Francisco Order, the San Francisco Court acknowledged that under *Heller* the Second Amendment has been found to guarantee the right of individuals to, *inter alia*, own and use firearms for self

---

[19] Available at http://michellawyers.com/wp-content/uploads/2013/12/Fyock-v-Sunnyvale_Emergency-Application-for-Injunction-Pending-Appeal_____1.pdf.

[20] Lyle Denniston, *Gun rights plea denied,* SCOTUSBLOG (Mar. 12, 2014), available at http://www.scotusblog.com/2014/03/new-test-of-gun-rights/

defense.[21] Furthermore, the San Francisco Court acknowledged that a total ban on a category of arms that are used for a lawful purpose would violate the Second Amendment.[22] This court then ignored the meaning of "category" to find that a total ban on all magazines with a certain capacity would not be a total ban on a category of arms because, according to the court, other categories of magazines would still be available. As will be discussed in Section V(f) hereof, the San Francisco Court's approach to permissible government infringement of individual rights would, if taken to its logical conclusion, form the legal basis for something as extreme as the prohibition of all homosexual sexual activity in the City of San Francisco. The San Francisco Court's reasoning seemed to be that a category of arms is no longer a category of arms if there are other categories of different arms extant.

---

[21] San Francisco Order, *supra* note 2 at 6.

[22] *Id.*, citing *Heller*.

From this torture of logic, the San Francisco Court next had to determine the level of scrutiny to apply to the San Francisco Magazine Ban.

According to the court in *United States v. Chovan*[23] "…the core of the Second Amendment is 'the right of law-abiding, responsible citizens to use arms in defense of hearth and home'"[24] and the level of scrutiny must be tied to how close a law comes to burdening that core.

The San Francisco Court glossed over the substance of this important point and chose instead to conclude that because there are other methods of self defense that would remain even if the San Francisco Magazine Ban were allowed to stand, the San Francisco Magazine Ban didn't

---

[23] 735 F.3d 1127 (9th Cir. 2013).

[24] *Chovan*, slip op. at 21, citing *Heller*.

burden a core element of the Second Amendment. Thus this court stated that intermediate, rather than strict, scrutiny would apply.

It is difficult to explain the arbitrary nature of the San Francisco Court's determination that the core of the Second Amendment was not burdened enough to warrant strict scrutiny. Citing to a study finding that the average number of rounds fired in self defense situations was 2.2, the San Francisco Court found that a 10 round magazine capacity would be sufficient in *most* cases for self defense purposes.

The study that was relied upon to find that the average number of rounds fired in self defense was inappropriate in several ways. First, the study was based on anecdotal or news stories published by a magazine to illustrate the use of firearms in self defense. Consequently, it only reflected incidents where the defender chose to go public with a report and it only included incidents where the defender was successful in defending him or herself.[25]

What this means in practical terms is that if a person were to have been assaulted by numerous assailants and had fired 10 rounds in self defense at the assailants, only to have been killed by the assailants as the defender ran out of ammunition due to the existing California law that prevents the sale or transfer of "large capacity magazines",[26] that

---

[25] *Allen Declaration* at note 10 in the San Francisco Order, and *see also* the study referred to therein, Claude Werner, "The Armed Citizen-A Five Year Analysis" (together with the Allen Declaration, the "Study"), stating "[t]his analysis does not present a view of the totality of armed self-defense in that non-positive outcomes were not available for inclusion in the database."

[26] This flaw also results in the exclusion of data where local restrictions on the sale and possession of guns were so onerous as to have resulted in a de facto ban on the possession of weapons in the home. For example, the City of San Francisco has a long history of attempting to ban civilian ownership of handguns and ammunition. *See* Don B. Kates and C.D. Michel, *Local Guns Bans in California: A Futile Exercise*,

41 U.S.F. L. Rev. 333 (2007) (examining, *inter alia*, the numerous handgun bans enacted by the City San Francisco over the course of the last four decades). As a result of San Francisco's enmity towards private firearms ownership many San Francisco residents find it nearly impossible to purchase firearms or ammunition. The result of this is that incidents like the 2012 massacre of five people at a house in San Francisco (hereinafter, the "2012 San Francisco Massacre"), where the assailant possessed nothing more than an edged weapon and/or hammer, aren't included in the study because the victims were effectively disarmed by the government. *See* Justin Berton, *S.F. Suspect Charged With Five Counts of Murder*, S.F. Chronicle March 28, 2012 (available at http://www.sfgate.com/crime/article/S-F-suspect-charged-with-5-counts-of-murder-3439280.php). Had one of the five victims possessed a firearm, the likelihood is that the assailant would have been stopped and the use of the firearm would have been added to the study.

While this argument is one the depends on many assumptions, the San Francisco Order was based on far more speculative and baseless assumptions, such as the court's claim that the need for more a magazine holding more than 10 rounds of ammunition will be "...rarer in a dense urban area like San Francisco where police will likely be alerted at the outset of gunfire and come to the aid of the victim". San Francisco Order, *supra* note 2 at 11. It is obvious that in a situation such as the 2012 San Francisco Massacre, the police did not prevent the slaughter of five innocent people and could not have responded in time to save the victims had they been alerted in some manner.

incident would not have been included in the data. This flaw means that a significant pool of data directly relevant to the purported basis for the San Francisco Magazine Ban were excluded from the study.

Second, the study used extreme assumptions in lieu of empirical evidence; to wit, the study admitted that it assumed that an average of shots fired in other incidents whenever the report stated that "shots were fired" without providing a specific count on the number of rounds fired. The underlying data upon which the study was based clearly stated that where more than two shots were fired, it usually meant that the person fired all the rounds in the weapon's magazine. Thus, it very likely undercounts the number of rounds fired in reported incidents.[27]

---

[27] *Allen Declaration* at note 10 in the San Francisco Order, stating "[w]hen the exact number of shots fired was not specified, we used the average for the most relevant incidents with known number of shots." This is a critical error, as the Claude Werner study found that

So not only are the data in the relied-upon study incomplete and not probative, using such a study is irrelevant in the question of whether the San Francisco Magazine Ban affects a core element of the Second Amendment. Self defense is the core element of the Second Amendment, according to *Chovan*, and whether or not the average person fires more or less than 10 rounds in the course of defending his or her self is simply background noise. There is no question that at times, citizens fire more than 10 rounds in self defense and that is the exercise of the core Second Amendment right.

Curiously, the study only examined the number of

"[w]hen more than 2 shots were fired, it generally appeared that the defender's initial response was to fire until empty", which for a revolver would generally be six rounds and for a semi automatic handgun with a detachable magazine would generally be between 8 and 20 rounds. *See* http://gunssavelives.net/self-defense/analysis-of-five-years-of-armed-encounters-with-data-tables/

rounds *fired* in the narrow categories of self defense incidents yet it shifted to the magazine *capacity* typically found in mass shootings in order to justify the ban on "large capacity magazines".[28] Because no data were included on the magazine *capacity* (as opposed to the number of rounds actually *fired* from the magazines) for the self defense incidents, as far as the court knew every single one of the self defense incidents involved "large capacity magazines". This is the danger in relying upon non-empirical studies. Were the studies used to have been "apples-to-apples", they would have compared the capacity (rather than the number of shots fired) of magazines used in self defense incidents to the capacity of magazines used in mass shootings.

Furthermore, while the San Francisco Court qualified the ill-effects of the San Francisco Magazine Ban

---

[28] San Francisco Order, supra note 2 at 8.

on putative "self defenders" by reminding us of the "ability of a self-defender to have two or more magazines" if more than 10 rounds are needed, [29] it utterly ignored the fact that criminal use of magazines in mass shooting incidents often involve the use of multiple magazines.[30] The Sandy Hook assailant changed magazines multiple times and still amassed an extraordinarily high number of casualties. It is thus unclear why the number of magazines a person uses is relevant to the question of whether a magazine is subject to the core protections of the Second Amendment.[31]

---

[29] *Id.* at 7.

[30] For example, in the Sandy Hook massacre, the assailant carried 10 magazines of .223 caliber ammunition and had used 7 of those magazines in full or part. *See* Lanza Report, *supra* note 15, at appendix "Weight of guns/ammo", available at http://www.scribd.com/doc/187058196/Newtown-Report-Weight-of-Guns-Ammo

[31] *See* the discussion of the Sunnyvale Order, supra note 2 at 9 for that court's explicit acknowledgement that a magazine is an "arm" for the purpose of the Second Amendment.

If it seems as though the San Francisco Court was simply randomly citing data that were contradictory and irrelevant, it's because that's exactly what the court was doing.

The applicability of constitutional rights is not based on averages, it is based on absolutes. Once a right is determined to exist for a defined constituency, either you have that right or you don't; it does not matter how far along the minimum and maximum values of a statistical table of those exercising the right you are placed. Anything else would mean that the Constitution gives you a right to defend yourself against 10 assailants, but not 11. This is clearly ludicrous, and it is certainly not for courts to say that a person has a right to defend him or herself against an average attack but not against an extraordinary attack.

(a) Intermediate Scrutiny as Applied in

the San Francisco Order

The San Francisco Court announced that it would apply intermediate scrutiny to the San Francisco Magazine ban(though it didn't explain the analysis that had to be performed thereunder), but in the same sentence it declared, with a conclusory and incomplete analysis, even under strict scrutiny the San Francisco Magazine Ban would not violate the Second Amendment.[32] Without providing any substantive analysis, the court concluded that the San Francisco Magazine Ban was the "least restrictive means" (a part of the standard test for strict scrutiny cases). The San Francisco Court, however, didn't say what the ban was the least restrictive means of accomplishing. It would appear that the subject matter was preventing mass

---

[32] San Francisco Order, *supra* note 2, at 7. However, it wasn't until page 9 of the San Francisco Order that the court provided some semblance of a rationale for stating that the San Francisco Magazine Ban would have also survived a strict scrutiny review.

murders.

The three problems with this are the San Francisco Court (1) didn't examine any alternatives to the San Francisco Magazine Ban; (2) didn't examine the frequency with which mass murders have been committed by means other than firearms with "large capacity magazines"; and (3) didn't provide any data on the total number of mass murders committed with firearms. Without this data and analysis, there was absolutely no way for the San Francisco Court to examine whether mass murders involving firearms (especially those with "large capacity magazines") occurred frequently enough to justify the draconian response of infringing on a constitutional right, let alone whether the ban was the least restrictive means of dealing with such a problem.

In many ways, the San Francisco Order reads as

though it was written by a court that had a predisposition to arrive at the ruling it made and was annoyed that it had to set forth any justification for it.

The San Francisco Court obliquely referred to the standards to be met in an intermediate scrutiny review by stating that it "…finds that the [San Francisco Magazine Ban] is substantially related to its interests in promoting public safety and preventing gun violence."[33] How did it find this? By concluding that the San Francisco Magazine Ban "prevents mass murderers from firing a larger number of rounds faster by depriving them of magazines with the capacity to accept more than ten rounds."[34]

Such a conclusion is, charitably put, nonsensical at

---

[33] *Id.* at 8.
[34] *Id.*

best.³⁵

As a start, a mass murderer will not be prevented from committing one crime (murder) simply because possession of a tool (magazines with capacities in excess of 10 rounds) used in the crime is a separate crime in and of itself. And as the San Francisco Court admitted, limiting the capacity of a magazine doesn't prevent a person from simply carrying with them numerous magazines so that the total number of rounds available to fire remains the same.

In the Sandy Hook massacre, the weight of each empty 30 round magazine was a mere 4 ounces.³⁶ A 10 round magazine weighs approximately 2 ounces and is

---

[35] The San Francisco Court, like the Sunnyvale Court, failed to satisfy its burden of proof with regard to the actual threat posed by "large capacity magazines". *See* discussion at Section VI hereof.

[36] *See* Lanza Report, *supra* note 15 at appendix "Weight of guns/ammo".

approximately 1/3rd the size of a 30 round magazine.^{37} It's obvious that there is virtually no difference in the size and weight between one 30 round magazine and three 10 round magazines. The majority of the weight difference between the magazines is in the actual ammunition, so whether it's 30 rounds in one magazine or divided among three magazines, the weight is approximately the same. The only conceivable reason for the San Francisco Court alleging that smaller magazines would prevent mass murders is the speculation that an unarmed victim would be able to tackle the assailant during the two to three seconds it takes for an average shooter to change magazines. ^{38}

---

[37] Information obtained from Magpul, Inc. technical service, contact information available at http://www.magpul.com/contactinfo.html.

[38] Jason Howerton, *Gun Experts: Limits on Magazine Size Will Only Slow Determined Killer Down by a Few Seconds* published at BLAZE.COM on Jan. 17, 2013, available at http://www.theblaze.com/stories/2013/01/17/gun-experts-limits-on-magazine-size-will-only-slow-determined-killer-down-by-a-few-seconds/ ("...a shooter needs 1.5 seconds to switch out a magazine

And for that incredibly speculative scenario, the San Francisco Court decided that the entire population of law abiding citizens of San Francisco should have their core Second Amendment rights infringed upon. Note, of course, that for the less speculative situation where a person would need more than 10 rounds to defend herself, the San Francisco Court dismissed the argument as being unlikely to occur, stating that "...those rare occasions [where a person needs more than 10 rounds to defend him or herself] must be weighed against the more frequent and documented occasions when a mass murderer with a gun holding eleven or more rounds empties the magazine and slaughters innocents".[39] In fact, though, as the 2012 San Francisco Massacre shows, the greater likelihood of a mass murder is where the victims have been effectively disarmed

---

and every five-round magazine takes about one to two seconds to unload...")

[39] San Francisco Order, *supra* note 15, at 11.

by San Francisco's onerous burdens on firearms possession.

More damming, the San Francisco Court dramatically exaggerated the actual risk of mass shootings. In a 2013 Congressional Research Service report[40] on mass shootings,[41] commissioned in response to the Sandy Hook massacre, it was found that over the course of the 30 years prior to the date of the report there had been a total of 547 deaths due to mass shootings in the United States.[42] This means that across 50 states and over 300,000,000 citizens,

---

[40] Bjelopera, J. P., Bagalman, E., Caldwell, S. W., Finklea, K. M., McCallion, G. PUBLIC MASS SHOOTINGS IN THE UNITED STATES: SELECTED IMPLICATIONS FOR FEDERAL PUBLIC HEALTH AND SAFETY POLICY (Congressional Research Service Report R43004) (2013) (hereinafter the "CRS Report"), available at https://www.fas.org/sgp/crs/misc/R43004.pdf

[41] Mass shootings were defined as "... incidents occurring in relatively public places, involving four or more deaths—not including the shooter(s)—and gunmen who select victims somewhat indiscriminately." *Id.* at Summary page 1.

[42] CRS Report, *supra* note 40, at 7.

there were approximately 18 fatalities from mass shootings each year. Even if we assume that all of the fatalities involved "large capacity magazines", this means that the odds in any year of San Francisco being the location of a mass shooting is infinitesimally small.[43]

For this extremely remote possibility, the San

---

[43] This is, of course, an unscientific estimate, but the San Francisco Order eschewed statistical analysis or any other form of quantification in its entirety, so the statistics presented here are a significant improvement in empirical analysis over what was presented in the San Francisco Order. Based on the average of 18 mass murder fatalities per year and approximately 300,000,000 residents in the United States, the annual rate of fatalities due to mass murder in the United States has been .000006%. The corresponding rate for San Francisco's population of approximately 800,000 is .000000016% per year. Based on the fact that a mass shooting, by definition, has to involve four victims, this would mean that there are approximately four mass shooting events per year in the United States. If we reduce the potential victim pool accordingly, from 300,0000,000 to 75,000,000, it still results in the odds of any of San Francisco's 800,000 residents being involved at approximately 01%. By any calculation, the odds of any of those four events occurring in San Francisco are well below 1%.

Francisco Court chose to uphold an infringement of the Second Amendment.

It is worth pointing out here that the San Francisco Court upheld the denial of a constitutional right under both intermediate and strict scrutiny based on the fact that law might prevent a mass murder that has less than a .01% chance of affecting a person in San Francisco in any given year.

(2) The Sunnyvale Order

While the Sunnyvale Order is a much more rigorous examination of the law and constitutional standards of review applicable to Second Amendment cases it still fails to adhere to the standards it so clearly explains.

The Sunnyvale Court engaged in a thorough review

of *Heller* and its progeny and went so far as to confirm several critical elements of those cases:

- "the Second Amendment extends to arms used for self defense both inside and outside the home";[44]
- "magazines having a capacity to accept more than ten rounds are in common use, and are therefore not dangerous and unusual" (meaning that they are subject to the protections of the Second Amendment) and the test for whether an arm is in common use is a national, not a local, one;[45]
- Under *Heller*, the test for whether an arm is protected by the Second Amendment is not whether such arm is commonly *used* for self

---

[44] Sunnyvale Order, *supra* note 2, at 6.

[45] *Id*. at 7.

defense; rather, the test is whether such arm is commonly *possessed*, without regard to the frequency of its use;[46]

- Ammunition magazines are "arms" for purposes of the Second Amendment;[47] and
- Therefore, ammunition magazines, including those with the capacity to accept more than 10 rounds, are subject to the protections of the Second Amendment.[48]

From that apparently rock-solid pronouncement, the Sunnyvale Court went about chipping away at the foundation of the Second Amendment. Like the San Francisco Court before it, the Sunnyvale Court applied intermediate scrutiny review to the Sunnyvale Magazine Ban. Unlike the San Francisco Court, however, the

---

[46] *Id.* at 8.

[47] *Id.* at 8-9.

[48] *Id.* at 9.

Sunnyvale Court explained the procedure for selecting the proper level of scrutiny.

If the court had found that the Sunnyvale Magazine Ban was a "destruction" of a Second Amendment right, it would have been *per se* invalid (i.e., no level of scrutiny would need to be selected as the law would be invalid without further inquiry).[49] If, however, the court had found that the Sunnyvale Magazine Ban burdened, but did not destroy, a Second Amendment right, it would have been subject to either strict or intermediate scrutiny, depending on the severity of the burden.

Ignoring the fact that it had just declared "large capacity magazines" to be arms protected under the Second Amendment and that the Sunnyvale Magazine Ban by its terms would effect a total ban (i.e., destruction of the right

---

[49] *Id.*

to possess the magazine) of those arms, the Sunnyvale Court conclusively declared that Sunnyvale Magazine Ban was a mere burden on the Second Amendment right.

The court wasn't finished with its logical gymnastics. It accepted an expert's testimony that "47% of all magazines owned are capable of holding more than 10 rounds"[50] but found that because this percentage was less than 50%, the "burden on the Second Amendment right is light"[51] and intermediate scrutiny was the appropriate level of scrutiny.

---

[50] *Id.* at 11.

[51] *Id.* at 12. Curiously, the Sunnyvale Court also argued that since "Large Capacity Magazines" were already banned from sale or transfer in California, they were "less preferred" and thus, apparently, not as "common". This, of course, flies in the face of the court's earlier acknowledgement that the standard was national, not local, when it comes to determining whether an arm is common. Furthermore, under this theory, California would be able to ban any item so long as it did so incrementally rather than at once.

(a) The Sunnyvale Order under Intermediate Scrutiny

The Sunnyvale Court then explained that under intermediate scrutiny, it would have to examine the stated objective of the challenged law to determine whether such objective was "significant, substantial or important"[52]. If the stated objective was significant, substantial or important, the court would then have to find that there was a "reasonable fit between the challenged regulation and the asserted objective."[53]

Assuming that the Sunnyvale Court had properly arrived at this point in its analysis (an assumption that this paper will rebut in Section VI hereog), it then takes a

---

[52] *Id.*

[53] *Id.* at 12-13.

logical u-turn in weighing the importance of the objective against the impact of the asserted objective. Claiming that the objective of the Sunnyvale Magazine Ban was "public safety and crime prevention"[54] (which, the court said, are "legitimate and compelling state interests" that can "outweigh an individual's liberty interest" in appropriate circumstances)[55] the Sunnyvale court then compared the arguments and testimony of each side's experts to conclude that the Sunnyvale Magazine Ban "*MAY*" partially achieve some elements of its stated objective.[56]

The Sunnyvale Court didn't find that the Sunnyvale Magazine Ban *WOULD* achieve its objectives, nor did it

---

[54] *Id.* at 13.

[55] *Id.* (citing *U.S. v. Salerno*, 481 U.S. 739 (1987) and *Schall v. Martin*, 467 U.S. 253 (1984)).

[56] "...even if the Sunnyvale law has minimal compliance among criminal firearm users and is difficult to enforce by police, it may still reduce gun crime by restricting the banned magazine's availability." Sunnyvale Order, *supra* note 2, at 14.

find that it would *LIKELY* achieve its objectives. The best the court could find was an entirely speculative and blatantly incomplete possibility that the infringement of constitutional rights by the City of Sunnyvale *MAY* reduce gun crime. In doing so, the Sunnyvale Court, like the San Francisco Court before it, dismissed every bit of evidence showing that the law would put law abiding residents in jeopardy and would likely have no appreciable effect on public safety and crime prevention, which were the stated objectives of the law, nor did it examine the frequency of occurrence of criminal use of "large capacity magazines" generally, so it, like the San Francisco Court, rendered an order that infringed a constitutional right without even examining whether there was a significant criminal or public safety problem being addressed by the ban.[57]

---

[57] *Id.* at 14-15, where the court makes the same mistakes as the San Francisco court with regard to the flaws in the Study that led it to undercount the lawful use of "large capacity magazines" in self defense. *See supra* notes 25 and 26.

Rather, the Sunnyvale Court, like the San Francisco Court, by justifying the ban simply because it *MIGHT* reduce gun related violence, implicitly used a standard of "if it even saves one life it justifies infringing a constitutional right."

The Sunnyvale Court also took into account the fact that voters in the City of Sunnyvale had approved the Sunnyvale Magazine Ban with a 66% majority, but failed to point out that the turnout in the election was less than 28% of registered voters, representing a mere 12,000 people speaking for the city's population of approximately 150,000 residents. [58]

Additionally, the Sunnyvale Court cited the need to protect police officers as justification for the Sunnyvale

---

[58] *See supra* note 17.

Magazine Ban, claiming the "large capacity magazines" somehow "present a special danger to law enforcement".[59] Curiously, however to support this claim the Sunnyvale Court referred to an incident from several years prior where a gunman with weapons having magazines with the capacity to accept more than 10 rounds was killed by police in Sunnyvale without a single police officer being harmed.[60]

---

[59] Sunnyvale Order, *supra* note 2, at 18.

[60] *See* Jeffrey F. Rosen, SANTA CLARA COUNTY DISTRICT ATTORNEY, "REPORT ON THE FATAL SHOOTING OF SHAREEF ALLMAN (Oct 6, 2011) (hereinafter, the "SCCDA Report", available at http://www.sccgov.org/sites/da/newsroom/newsreleases/Documents/OIS-ShareefAllman_2.pdf. Interestingly, this report shows that the gunman had a Glock .40 caliber handgun with a magazine capacity of 10 rounds or less (SCCDA Report at 11), so this handgun would have still been legal even if the Sunnyvale Magazine Ban had been in effect at the time of the incident. The other weapons used by the gunman were both so-called "assault weapons", which, if they were fitted with magazines having a capacity in excess of 10 rounds, would have been illegal to own or possess under California law, even if the magazines had been legal to possess (this is because under California law, even a so-called "off-list lower" rifle, which resembles an AK47 or AR15 type

The District Court Orders were similar in many respects, including their reliance on the statistic that "…individuals acting in self defense fire 2.1-2.2 shots on average"[61] and their justification for each Magazine Ban as

---

rifle and is legal to possess in California, becomes an illegal "assault weapon" once a magazine with a capacity of more than 10 rounds is attached to it, even if that magazine was legal to possess otherwise. See Marc A. Greendorfer, *People v. Zondorak: California's Attack on the Second Amendment* . 17 Chap. L. Rev. Online 1, 5-6 (2014)). So under any circumstance, the gunman, who didn't harm police officers, was already violating then-existing law by his possession of the weapons, which clearly didn't stop him from committing his crime. The zealous protection of government officials, to the point that it is used as a basis to deny a constitutional right of the population at large, is likely also a violation of the Constitution's Nobility Clauses. See, e.g., Marc A. Greendorfer, *Restoring Nobility to the Constitution: A Modern Approach to a Founding Principle*, (publication in the Akron Law Review forthcoming, currently available at http://papers.ssrn.com/sol3/papers.cfm?abstract_id=2335822) (2013).

[61] Sunnyvale Order, *supra* note 2, at 14; a similar use of this statistic is found in the San Francisco Order, supra note 2, at 7.

a means of protecting the lives of police officers.[62] This is indeed curious, since studies have found that the average number of shots fired by law enforcement officers is actually lower than 2.2. [63] The only thing that can be

---

[62] San Francisco Order, *supra* note 2, at 11 and Sunnyvale Order, *supra* note 2, at 18 mimic each other in saying that each city has an interest in "protecting the ...safety of its police officers."

[63] NEW YORK CITY POLICE DEPARTMENT, ANNUAL FIREARMS DISCHARGE REPORT 2011 (Aug. 2012) at page 24, available at http://www.nyc.gov/html/nypd/downloads/pdf/analysis_and_planning/nypd_annual_firearms_discharge_report_2011.pdf (" When working with such a small number of incidents, officers, and rounds fired, typical use of means and medians can lead to false conclusions. Additionally, as noted above, a single incident can significantly skew averages. For this reason, with small samples, the mode can be most revelatory [see Figure A.10]. The mode for the number of shots fired by police is one.") The same average (one shot fired) was reported in the 2012 version of the report (http://www.nyc.gov/html/nypd/downloads/pdf/analysis_and_planning/nypd_annual_firearms_discharge_report_2012.pdf at page 20). While these data are only for the New York City Police Department, they are far more accurate and empirical than the 2.1-2.2 civilian data relied upon by the District Courts, as the New York City Police Department logs every shot fired by an officer. The civilian statistics were anecdotal. Furthermore, since the New York City Police

gleaned from the District Court's arguments is that it is citizens, not law enforcement, who have the greater demonstrated need for "large capacity magazines" yet only law enforcement officials are allowed to lawfully posses them.

In both District Court Orders, neither city presented empirical evidence showing that "large capacity magazines" presented a risk to their respective cities or to the nation as a whole, neither city quantified the magnitude of any such risk, if it did exist, or compared it to other risks that were not subjected to draconian bans, and neither city could refute the fact that "large capacity magazines" are arms subject to the protections of the Second Amendment.

Department is the largest municipal force in the country, with over 35,000 sworn personnel serving the largest population center in the country, these data are a reliable representation of police shootings generally. *See* Brian Reeves, *Local Police Departments 2007*, U.S. DEP'T OF JUSTICE, BUREAU OF JUSTICE STATISTICS (Dec. 2010), NCJ 231174 Table 1, available at http://www.bjs.gov/content/pub/pdf/lpd07.pdf.

Yet, each District Court Order upheld the respective Magazine Ban.

Quite simply, there is no precedent in constitutional jurisprudence for the District Court Orders sweeping, unjustified denial of enumerated individual rights.

iii) Precedent in Cases Involving Government Infringement of Constitutional and Other Rights

1. Same Sex Marriage

Perhaps no case in recent history relating to the protections afforded to individuals in the face of majority rule has garnered as much public debate and scholarly attention as the battle over California's Proposition 8.

Proposition 8 was a voter initiative to amend the State of California's constitution so that the only marriages recognized by the State of California would be marriages between a man and a woman. The amendment was approved by over 52% of those casting votes in the election (a margin of victory representing approximately 600,000 California voters).[64]

Proposition 8 didn't criminalize same sex relationships or same sex sexual activity. The only thing it did was, in a state that otherwise provided equal legal standing for same sex couples, deprive them of being recognized as married.[65]

---

[64] *See* http://www.sos.ca.gov/elections/sov/2008-general/maps/returns/props/prop-8.htm for data on the number of votes cast and the margin of victory for Proposition 8.

[65] *See Perry v. Brown*, 671 F.3d 1052, 1064 (9th Cir. 2012) ("California had already extended to committed same-sex couples both the incidents of marriage and the official designation of 'marriage' and

California has a long history of restricting the recognition of marriage to opposite sex unions. The first formal act was a 1977 legislative act defining marriage as only between a man and a woman.[66] Then, in 2000, to assure that the effects of the 1977 legislative act could not be altered (since California law does not allow the State's legislature to amend voter approved initiatives), an initiative was approved by California's voters to preserve the traditional definition of marriage.[67] Only after a small group of San Francisco activists challenged the 2000 initiative and persuaded the California Supreme Court to overrule the will of the voters in early 2008 was same sex marriage permitted, albeit briefly, in California.

Proposition 8's only effect was to take away that ... designation while leaving in place all of its incidents.")

[66] *Id.* at 1065.

[67] *Id.*

Legalized same sex marriages lasted for a grand total of 143 days, during which time approximately 18,000 same sex couples become married in California, before Proposition 8 was approved by California's voters and the state constitution was thereby amended to once again affirm that only marriages between men and women would be recognized in California. Proposition 8 did not affect the same sex marriages that had already been recognized in California to that point.[68]

The proponents of Proposition 8 argued that marriage had a very specific traditional meaning throughout human history and expanding it to include same sex unions would have a host of enumerated ill effects on

---

[68] *Id.* at 1068. In this way, Proposition 8 was like California's state-wide "large capacity magazine" ban from 1999, which did not require the relinquishment of such magazines that had been acquired prior to the effective date of the 1999 ban.

society and the institution of marriage.[69]

The 9th Circuit applied the lowest level of constitutional scrutiny, "rational basis", to Proposition 8,[70] describing the test as "if a law neither burdens a fundamental right nor targets a suspect class, we will uphold the legislative classification so long as it bears a rational relation to some legitimate end."[71]

If grand juries are so loathe to reject the call for indictment as to give rise to the aphorism that they would indict a ham sandwich if one were presented to them,[72]

---

[69] *See* Brief of Petitioners at 31-55, *Hollingsworth v. Perry*, 671 F.3d 1052 (9th Cir. 2012) (No. 12-144).

[70] *Perry, supra* note 65, at 1082.

[71] *Id.*, citing *Romer v. Evans*, 517 U.S 620, 631 (1996).

[72] *See* Glenn Harlan Reynolds, *Ham Sandwich Nation: Due Process When Everything Is a Crime*, 113 COLUM. L. REV. Sidebar 102 at note 15 (2013), http://www.columbialawreview.org/ham-sandwich-nation_Reynolds.

laws that are subject to a rational basis review are veritable constitutional ham sandwiches.[73] By all standards, Proposition 8 should have been upheld, simply because the rational basis review asks for so little to justify the continued existence of a law.

Yet Proposition 8 was not only found to be unconstitutional, the 9th Circuit thoroughly castigated the majority of voters in California for having voiced their preferences with regard to marriage.

Proclaiming "Proposition 8 works a meaningful harm to gays and lesbians, by denying to their committed

---

[73] *See* Kenji Yoshino, *The New Equal Protection*, 124 Harv. L. Rev. 747 (2011) at 756 ("...rational basis review generally results in validation of state action") (*quoting* LAURENCE H. TRIBE, AMERICAN CONSTITUTIONAL LAW § 16-2, at 1442-43 (2d ed. 1988) "The traditional deference both to legislative purpose and to legislative selections among means continues ... to make the rationality requirement largely equivalent to a strong presumption of constitutionality.").

lifelong relationships the societal status conveyed by the designation of 'marriage,' and this harm must be justified by some legitimate state interest"[74] the 9th Circuit set forth four of Proposition 8's purported goals for review: (1) furthering California's interest in childrearing and responsible procreation, (2) proceeding with caution before making significant changes to marriage, (3) protecting religious freedom, and (4) preventing children from being taught about same-sex marriage in schools.[75]

As a preliminary issue, it is important to note that the 9th Circuit chose to not incorporate the conclusion of the District Court below it that there is a fundamental right to same sex marriage.[76]

---

[74] *Perry, supra* note 65, at 1081.

[75] *Id.* at 1086.

[76] *Id.* at 1082. Opposite sex marriage has previously been found to be a fundamental right that is protected, inter alia, by the Constitution's Due Process and Equal Protection clauses. *See, e.g., Loving v. Virginia* 388 U.S. 1 (1967). This is an important point in considering the status

This paper will not re-argue *Perry* or engage in an in-depth analysis of the 9th Circuit's treatment of each of the four purported goals of Proposition 8. Instead, *Perry* is discussed here as a reference point for the threshold considerations that can tip the scale under various levels of constitutional scrutiny. For that purpose, the 9th Circuit's analysis of the second purported Proposition 8 goal, "proceeding with caution before making significant changes to marriage", is used for illustrative purposes.

The *Perry* court started its dismissal of this goal by incorrectly stating that "this rationale, too, bears no connection to the reality of Proposition 8. The amendment was enacted after the State had provided same-sex couples

---

of the Magazine Bans as an infringement of an enumerated right under the Constitution and comparing the court's treatment of it to the treatment of rights that are not enumerated or fundamental, such as the right to same sex marriage.

the right to marry and after more than 18,000 couples had married...."[77]

The State of California acts through its legislature and the direct vote of its citizens via the initiative process, not through its courts. The *Perry* court utterly ignored the fact that the State of California had consistently acted to ***deny*** same sex couples the right to marry. It did so in 1977, when the California legislature revised the state's marriage code to read "[m]arriage is a personal relation arising out of a civil contract between a man and a woman, to which the consent of the parties capable of making that contract is necessary."[78] The voters of California subsequently reiterated their rejection of same sex marriage in 2000 through their approval of Proposition 22.[79] Only after a group of San Francisco activists persuaded the California

---

[77] *Perry,* supra note 65, at 1089.

[78] Cal. Stats. 1977, ch. 339, § 1.

[79] Codified at Cal. Fam. Code § 308.5.

Supreme Court to strike down Proposition 22 in 2008 was same sex marriage allowed in California, and once again, the voters of California decisively rejected that court's ruling by approving Proposition 8 less than six months later.[80]

In the election deciding Proposition 8, over 79% of California's registered voters participated, a rate that was higher than any other statewide general election in the prior 32 years.[81] By any standard, the voter participation rate clearly indicated that Proposition 8 was the clear will of the State's voters.

Whatever was happening in California prior to the

---

[80] *Perry, supra* note 65, at 1065.

[81] *See* California Secretary of State *Statement of Vote, November 4, 2008 General Election* at 4. Prior to the 2008 election's 79.42% participation rate there had not been a participation rate in excess of 79% since the 1976 election's participation rate of 81.53%. The next highest participation rate was 77.24% in the 1980 election. Id.

Perry decision, it was the unelected judiciary of the State of California, not the people, nor their representative in the legislature, who "provided same-sex couples the right to marry…."

Thus, one would have to suspend disbelief (or, perhaps, not even be sentient) to find, as the *Perry* court did, that the people of California weren't interested in proceeding cautiously with regard to recognizing same sex marriages. In fact, the people of California were quite clearly opposed to recognizing same sex marriage. The California courts, however, had an opposite point of view.

The *Perry* court said that the question it had to answer was whether the "[p]eople of California have legitimate reasons for enacting a constitutional amendment that serves only to take away from same-sex couples the right to have their lifelong relationships dignified by the official status of 'marriage'....".[82] The answer is obvious: Through Proposition 8, millions of California voters, representing a majority of those voting, reacted to the invalidation of an existing law by an insular group of four California judges by reaffirming their desire to deny recognition of same sex marriages. Since the standard of review was rational basis, it should have been sufficient for the *Perry* court to end its inquiry at this point since both a legitimate interest (taking a deliberate approach to an evolving societal standard) and a rational relationship between the law and the interest existed. Instead, the *Perry* court granted de-facto suspect class status to same sex marriages (without finding a constitutional right to same sex marriages) in order to arrive at its conclusion that Proposition 8 violated the Equal Protection Clause.

When viewed in its entirety, *Perry* stands for the

---

[82] *Perry, supra* note 65, at 1079.

proposition that even for rights that are neither fundamental nor substantive, nor enumerated in the Constitution,[83] nor even applicable to the vast majority of society,[84] courts will go so far as to reject the clear and repeatedly stated will of the people, even if it means judicial intervention to create a right that is primarily symbolic.[85]

---

[83] Even the *Perry* court acknowledged that Proposition 8 did not discriminate against same sex couples in any way other than withholding the status of "marriage"—all of the legal incidents of marriage were specifically granted to such couples under California's domestic partnership law (*Perry, supra* note 65, at 1077) and the actual effect of Proposition 8 was "symbolic" (*Id.* at 1078).

[84] It is not possible to estimate the total number of same sex couples that seek the status of marriage, but in the first full year that same sex marriages were legal in the State of New York, approximately 5% of all marriages were known to be between same sex couples. *See* Drew Desilver, *How many same-sex marriages in the U.S.? At least 71,165, probably more* PEW RESEARCH CENTER, June 26, 2013, available at http://www.pewresearch.org/fact-tank/2013/06/26/how-many-same-sex-marriages-in-the-u-s-at-least-71165-probably-more/.

[85] Because the United States Supreme Court did not reach the merits of *Perry* in its 2013 decision in the case (the Supreme Court ruled that the appellants didn't have standing, which had the effect of leaving in place the District Court's decision that Proposition 8 was

(2) Speech and Assembly Restrictions under the First Amendment

In evaluating the legal justifications for a total or partial infringement of an enumerated constitutional right predicated on the state's interests in health and safety of citizens, it is particularly helpful to examine how the

---

unconstitutional-*see Hollingsworth v. Perry*, 570 U.S. ___ (2013)) this paper will not examine the Supreme Court decision. Similarly, in a contemporaneously decided case on the topic of federal recognition of same sex marriages (*United States v. Windsor*, 570 U.S. ___ (2013)), the Supreme Court declined to rule on whether there was a constitutionally protected right to same sex marriage; rather, the case was nominally decided on federalism grounds, with the Court stating that the federal government could not undermine state marriage laws by enforcing federal laws that negatively impacted same sex couples married in states allowing same sex marriage. *Windsor*, 570 U.S., at 22–26 (slip op.). Because the Supreme Court declined to directly address the issue of same sex marriage under the Constitution, the *Windsor* decision is not illustrative for purposes of this paper's discussion of *Perry*.

Supreme Court has addressed limitations on the First Amendment rights of speech and assembly.

(a) Abortion Clinic Protest Restrictions

In Hill v. Colorado[86] the United States Supreme Court upheld a Colorado ordinance restricting First Amendment speech rights within 100 yards of abortion clinics and health facilities. Admitting that the Colorado ordinance was a restriction on speech, the court's decision hinged on the fact that the restrictions were content neutral and designed to protect the interest Colorado had in protecting the health and safety of its citizens, particularly those entering a medical facility for treatment.

The court employed a form of intermediate scrutiny, over the objections of the dissent, to find that the

---

[86] 530 U.S. 703 (2000).

restrictions were "narrowly tailored" in that they only prohibited a person from engaging in the restricted speech if that person was within 100 yards of an abortion clinic and less than 8 feet from any particular person entering the clinic, thus still allowing the speaker to communicate his or her message to the intended audience.[87]

The holding in *Hill* has to be contrasted to the holding in Schenck v. Pro-Choice Network of Western New York.[88] In *Schenck*, the United States Supreme Court found that while a prohibition on demonstrations within a fixed 15 foot buffer zone around the entrance to an abortion clinic was permissible, a floating 15 foot buffer zone around any individual as she entered or exited a clinic was an impermissible infringement on the demonstrators' First Amendment speech rights. The court, employing a form of

---

[87] *Id.* at 726-727.
[88] 519 U.S. 357 (1997).

intermediate scrutiny,[89] explained that the floating buffer zone effectively stopped demonstrators from communicating with their intended audience and thus "burden[ed] more speech than is necessary to serve the relevant governmental interests."[90]

In neither *Hill* nor *Schenck* were the restrictions

---

[89] *Id.* at 369 (the court weighed "...whether the speech restrictions (i) were content neutral, (ii) were narrowly tailored to serve a significant government interest, and (iii) left open ample alternative channels for communication of the information.").

[90] *Id.* at 377. As in *Hill*, the government interest in *Schenck* was public safety. The *Schenck* court noted that without buffer zones, demonstrations often devolved into physical altercations between the demonstrators and those supporting the abortion clinic patients. See, also, McCullen v. Coakley (573 U.S. ___ (2014)(slip op.)), where the Supreme Court struck down a Massachusetts law that expanded a no speech zone to 35 feet from 18 feet from abortion clinics. Indeed, the Supreme Court responded to Massachusetts's claim that it needed to expand the no speech zone because enforcement of the 18 foot zone was too difficult by pointing out that the solution was to make greater efforts to enforce the existing zone rather than suppress protected speech. *Id.* at 27.

on speech absolute prohibitions on any aspect of First Amendment rights. The prohibitions still allowed the affected parties to engage in exactly the conduct that they desired to engage in, within very limited time, place and manner restrictions.

Hill and *Schenck* show that under intermediate scrutiny an absolute ban on constitutionally protected conduct will not be upheld. It would have been easy for the *Schenck* court to have found that protesting within such close confines at or near an abortion clinic was simply a subset of speech and the protesters remained free to communicate their messages in public at all places other than an abortion clinic. *Schenck*, however, explicitly rejected the notion that the continued right to exercise a subset of a protected right is a permissible substitute for the exercise of all protected aspects of that right.

(b) Gang Injunctions

Chicago v. Morales,[91] a United States Supreme Court decision on the permissibility of a local restriction on assembly by suspected gang members, is even more illustrative. In striking down a local ordinance that prohibited suspected gang members from gathering in public[92] the Supreme Court, while acknowledging that gangs were significant contributors to an epidemic of street violence and, in particular, homicides, plaguing the City of

---

[91] 527 U.S. 41 (1999).

[92] The ordinance consisted of four parts: "First, the police officer must reasonably believe that at least one of the two or more persons present in a "`public place' " is a "`criminal street gang membe[r].' " Second, the persons must be "`loitering,' " which the ordinance defines as "`remain[ing] in any one place with no apparent purpose.' " Third, the officer must then order "`all' " of the persons to disperse and remove themselves "`from the area.' " Fourth, a person must disobey the officer's order. If any person, whether a gang member or not, disobeys the officer's order, that person is guilty of violating the ordinance." *Id.* at 47.

Chicago, stated that the ordinance could not pass constitutional muster in that it was a "...criminal law that contains no *mens rea* requirement....and infringes on constitutionally protected rights."[93]

While in Morales the lower court found that the ordinance violated the First Amendment right of assembly of the plaintiffs, the Supreme Court declined to rule on that

---

[93] *Id.* at 55. While the lower court found that the ordinance violated the First Amendment right of assembly of the plaintiffs, the Supreme Court declined to rule on that element and instead found that because the ordinance did not specify particular conduct that would give rise to criminal liability, it was constitutionally vague. *Id.* at 51. While there are significant substantive differences between a ruling that a law is unconstitutionally vague and a ruling that a law infringes upon an individual's First Amendment rights, given the explanation provided by the Supreme Court for its ruling, it would be hard to imagine any formulation of the subject law that would be specific enough to no longer be constitutionally vague yet still be broad enough to have the law's desired effect of stopping assembly of wide groups of people who were only suspected of gang affiliations. Thus, while the Supreme Court didn't explicitly affirm the lower court's ruling of a First Amendment infringement, as precedent for gang injunction laws it has the same effect.

element and instead found that because the ordinance did not specify particular conduct that would give rise to criminal liability, it was constitutionally vague.[94] While there are significant substantive differences between a ruling that a law is unconstitutionally vague and a ruling that a law infringes upon an individual's First Amendment rights, given the explanation provided by the United States Supreme Court for its ruling, it would be hard to imagine any formulation of the subject law that would be specific enough to no longer be constitutionally vague yet still be broad enough to have the law's desired effect of stopping assembly of wide groups of people who were only suspected of gang affiliations. Thus, while the United States Supreme Court didn't explicitly affirm the lower court's ruling of a First Amendment infringement, as precedent for gang injunction laws it has the same effect.

---

[94] *Id.* at 51.

It would be hard to ignore the similarities between the Chicago ordinance and the Magazine Bans. The Chicago ordinance didn't apply only to convicted gang members; it allowed police to presume that an individual had engaged in and/or had the requisite mental state that is a prerequisite to a finding of criminal conduct based on otherwise non-criminal conduct of the suspect. The *Morales* court even acknowledged that the solution to the problem of violent crime resided within the existing Chicago laws that prohibited actual criminal conduct.[95] In short, both the Chicago ordinance and the Magazine Bans presume illegal conduct simply because of an incidental, facial appearance and both constitute a total ban on protected conduct as a result of that presumption.

If one were to put the *Morales* decision in layman's terms, it would sound something like "a law that

---

[95] *Id.* at 52, note 17.

broadly prohibits constitutionally protected conduct simply because some criminal activity may be associated with vague elements of that conduct is constitutionally infirm."

(c) Violent Video Game Restrictions

In 2005, California Governor Arnold Schwarzenegger signed into law Assembly Bill 1179 (hereinafter, "AB1179")[96], a prohibition on the sale or rental of video games with violent themes to minors. AB1179 was the second attempt by then-California State Senator Leland Yee to ban the sale of violent video games. Like many of California's recent firearms laws,[97] AB1179 was

---

[96] California Assembly Bill 1179 (2005), Cal. Civ. Code Ann. §§1746-1746.5 (West 2009).

[97] Senator Leland Yee was indicted in California on charges of, *inter alia*, firearms trafficking in March 2014. *See* http://www.sfgate.com/file/757/757-complaint_affidavit_14-70421-nc.pdf for a copy of the indictment (hereinafter, the "Yee Indictment"). As is detailed in the Yee Indictment, Senator Yee was working with international arms dealers to facilitate the purchase and shipment of "large capacity magazine" weapons, "assault weapons"

and shoulder fired missiles in exchange for campaign contributions that were made to Senator Yee. Yee Indictment at 84-86. Prior to this indictment, Senator Yee had been hailed by many anti-Second Amendment groups for his legislative attempts to effectively ban the private ownership of virtually all firearms. See, e.g., Senator Yee's 2006 press release, *Brady Campaign to Honor Yee for Violence Prevention* available at http://sd08.senate.ca.gov/news/2006-08-04-brady-campaign-honor-yee-violence-prevention#sthash.LW7AWrDC.dpuf (announcing that the Brady Campaign to Prevent Gun Violence, a leading anti-Second Amendment organization, had named Senator Yee to its "Gun Violence Prevention Honor Roll" and listing a number of Senator Yee's gun-banning legislative accomplishments.) Until the time of his indictment, Senator Yee remained a leader of the California legislature's anti-Second Amendment efforts. While this is not to say that all firearms related legislation is borne of political corruption and sold to the public with false claims of concern for public safety, Senator Yee's indictment is a stark example of the disingenuous arguments made by those who push ever more draconian firearms regulations. It is also an example of what the *Brown* court warned about in questioning "...whether the government is in fact pursuing the interest it invokes" with Senator Yee's AB1179. If nothing else, the Senator Yee gun trafficking scandal gives us reason to closely examine the justifications for gun regulations, including the conclusory and illogical studies purporting to document the risks of "large capacity magazines" that were relied upon in the District Court Orders, as well as the motivations for introduced by Senator Yee with the Legislative findings proclaiming that the law was needed as a matter of public safety:

> *(a) Exposing minors to depictions of violence in video games, including sexual and heinous violence, makes those minors more likely to experience feelings of aggression, to experience a reduction of activity in the frontal lobes of the brain, and to exhibit violent antisocial or aggressive behavior.*

> *(b) Even minors who do not commit acts of violence suffer psychological harm from prolonged exposure to violent video games.*

---

politicians who support bans, which ultimately result in black markets like the one Senator Yee profited from.

> *(c) The state has a compelling interest in preventing violent, aggressive, and antisocial behavior, and in preventing psychological or neurological harm to minors who play violent video games.*[98]

The video game industry objected to the draconian elimination of its products from one of the industry's most lucrative market segments and in Brown v. Entertainment Merchants Ass'n., 564 U.S. ____ (2011), challenged the constitutionality of AB1179.

The challenge to AB1179 centered on the fact that the AB1179 ban was a content based[99] restriction on

---

[98] Section 1 of the *Legislative Counsel's Digest for AB1179*, available at http://leginfo.legislature.ca.gov/faces/billNavClient.xhtml?bill_id=200520060AB1179.

[99] That is, video games with specific violent content were subject to the ban.

minors' First Amendment's Free Speech Clause rights.[100] California attempted to defend AB1179 by claiming that the ban was permissible as it was directed solely at minors and was necessary because video games are "interactive" and thus have a greater likelihood of becoming de-facto violence simulators.

Justice Scalia quickly dispatched California's claims, re-affirming that aside from cases of obscenity, which are in turn limited to cases involving sexual content,[101] minors have First Amendment Free Speech

---

[100] Brown v. Entertainment Merchants Ass'n, 564 U.S. ____ (2011) (slip op. at 2). For a discussion on the applicability of the First Amendment to video games generally, *see Interactive Digital Software Ass'n. v. St. Louis County, Missouri*, 329 F.3d 954(8th Cir. 2003) ("whether we believe the advent of violent video games adds anything of value to society is irrelevant; guided by the first amendment, we are obliged to recognize that 'they are as much entitled to the protection of free speech as the best of literature.'")

[101] *Brown, supra* note 100, slip op. at 5.

rights that are substantially similar to adults'.[102] Furthermore, Justice Scalia noted that the interactive nature of modern video games was, in fact, not substantively different from the interactive nature decades-old children's books and literature in general.[103] With the foregoing matters established, Justice Scalia announced that AB1179 could be upheld only if it passed a strict scrutiny review, with California showing that there is an "actual problem in need of solving" where the infringement of the First Amendment is "actually necessary to the solution".[104]

In fact, the United States Supreme Court found that California had utterly failed to satisfy either prong of the strict scrutiny test. Further clarifying the standard that California would have to meet, Justice Scalia set the initial

---

[102] *Id.* at 7 (citing to Erznoznik v. City of Jacksonville, 422 U.S. 205 (1975))

[103] *Brown, supra* note 100, slip op.. at 10-11.

[104] *Id.* at 12.

threshold at "a direct causal link between violent video games and harm to minors."[105] Justice Scalia noted that the links presented by California were studies that had been universally rejected by other courts[106] and were "...based on **correlation**, not evidence of **causation**... and most of the studies suffer from significant, admitted flaws in methodology."[107] In addition, the Supreme Court found that AB1179 was "...wildly underinclusive when judged against its asserted justification...[which] raises serious doubts about whether the government is in fact pursuing the interest it invokes, rather than disfavoring a particular speaker of viewpoint."[108]

If this description from *Brown* sounds familiar, it is likely because it could also be used to describe the

---

[105] *Id.*

[106] *Id.*

[107] *Id.* (emphasis added).

[108] *Id.* at 14.

studies and methodologies employed by the San Francisco and Sunnyvale courts in the Magazine Bans, which were primarily anecdotal and fatally flawed in methodology that had the effect of ignoring data that would have provided evidence for the prevalence of the lawful possession and use of "large capacity magazines" in self defense situations.

In *Brown*, California argued that it did not have to show a direct causal link between video games and violence among minors as a result of Turner Broadcasting System, Inc. v. FCC,[109] which held that Congress could rely on predicative judgments in lieu of establishing direct causal links when making laws that infringed upon constitutional rights. The *Brown* court, however, pointed out that *Turner* was a case decided under an intermediate scrutiny review, so the lower level of proof from that case did not apply in the instant case, which was being reviewed

---

[109] 512 U.S. 622 (1994).

under strict scrutiny. More important, in *Turner*, Justice Kennedy qualified the Court's deference to Congress' use of predictive judgments with a critical caveat:

> *That Congress' predictive judgments are entitled to substantial deference does not mean, however, that they are insulated from meaningful judicial review altogether. On the contrary, we have stressed in First Amendment cases that the deference afforded to legislative findings does "not foreclose our independent judgment of the facts bearing on an issue of constitutional law." Sable Communications of Cal., Inc. v. FCC, 492 U.S. 115, 129 (1989); see also Landmark Communications, Inc. v. Virginia, 435 U.S. 829, 843 (1978). This obligation to exercise independent judgment when First Amendment rights are implicated is not a license to reweigh the evidence de novo, or to replace*

Congress' factual predictions with our own. Rather, it is to assure that, in formulating its judgments, Congress has drawn reasonable inferences based on substantial evidence. See Century Communications Corp. v. FCC, 835 F.2d 292, 304 (CADC 1987) ("[W]hen trenching on first amendment interests, even incidentally, the government must be able to adduce either empirical support or at least sound reasoning on behalf of its measures").[110]

The studies used to support AB1179 were quite extensive and, as the *Brown* dissent argued, persuasive in showing a strong connection between violent video games and criminal activity. Justice Breyer, in his dissent, engaged in his own study to document what he found to be not only a strong correlation between the playing of violent

---

[110] *Turner, supra* note 109, at 666.

video games and violent activity in society[111] but also a causal connection. Even with this level of empirical support, the Supreme Court found that the studies were still too speculative to be relied upon.[112]

In *Brown*, the Supreme Court found that the threshold to infringe on a constitutional right[113] is much higher than simply showing a correlation between two things. Empirical evidence of causation, not just correlation, is what must first be established by the government if it seeks to deprive a person of such a right.

---

[111] *Brown, supra* note 100, at 12-17 (Breyer, J., dissenting)

[112] *Id.* at footnote 8.

[113] In *Brown* the constitutional right in question was a First Amendment right. In *Heller* Justice Scalia pointed towards First Amendment jurisprudence for guidance in establishing the framework of Second Amendment standards, so this paper argues that government must establish causation, not just correlation, when it seeks to regulate arms based on public safety concerns. *See* Section VI hereof for this argument.

(3) Government Responses to the AIDS Epidemic

In the early 1980s a deadly epidemic swept across the world, ultimately killing over 35 million people worldwide between 1981 and 2014.[114] Of that number, over 636,000 of the casualties have been in the United States.[115] What has been so deadly that it had a casualty count in the United States that exceeds all United States military casualties from World War I to the present?[116]

---

[114] See *Global Statistics* at the UNITED STATES DEPARTMENT OF HEALTH & HUMAN SERVICES AIDS INFORMATION website (hereinafter, the "AIDS Informational Website"), available at http://aids.gov/hiv-aids-basics/hiv-aids-101/global-statistics/

[115] Id. at *U.S. Statistics* page, available at http://aids.gov/hiv-aids-basics/hiv-aids-101/statistics/.

[116] The total number of United States military deaths in all wars from World War I to the present is approximately 600,000. *See* Anne Leland and Mari-Jana Oboroceanu, *American War and Military Operations Casualties: Lists and Statistics* (Congressional Research Service Report RL32492) at 9 (Feb. 26, 2010), available at http://www.fas.org/sgp/crs/natsec/RL32492.pdf. The total number of

AIDS.[117]

deaths in connection with AIDS in the United States as of 2013 was 636,000. See the AIDS Informational Website, *supra* note 114, at "U.S. Statistics" (available at http://aids.gov/hiv-aids-basics/hiv-aids-101/statistics/index.html#ref3 and stating " An estimated 15,529 people with an AIDS diagnosis died in 2010, and approximately 636,000 people in the United States with an AIDS diagnosis have overall.")

[117] *See* the AIDS Informational Website, *supra* note 114, at "What is HIV/AIDS", available at http://aids.gov/hiv-aids-basics/hiv-aids-101/what-is-hiv-aids/. ("Acquired Immunodeficiency Syndrome is the final stage of HIV infection. People at this stage of HIV disease have badly damaged immune systems, which put them at risk for opportunistic infections"). Though HIV and AIDS are distinct medical terms, for purposes of this paper, especially with regard to fatality data, the term AIDS will be used to refer to both HIV and AIDS. The title of this paper is an homage to the book *And the Band Played On: Politics, People and the AIDS Epidemic* by Randy Shilts (St. Martin's Press 1987). Shilts chronicled the massive human toll of the AIDS epidemic, ultimately succumbing to the disease himself, yet never advocated for bans on behavior or activity as a response to the disease. Thus, while the title of Shilts' book was a reference to the lack of action to fight AIDS, the title of this paper is a commentary on the unprecedented and antithetical nature of the push, primarily from politically liberal corners (such as the Law Center to Prevent Gun

In the United States, while no major city was spared from the AIDS epidemic, New York City and San Francisco were particularly hard hit.[118] As the scope and lethality of the AIDS crisis began to unfold and thousands of new victims were reported, each city attempted to formulate a response.

Though the medical community's understanding of HIV and AIDS was in its infancy, shortly after the AIDS epidemic became a mainstay of public discussion it was believed that a prime contributor to the deadly disease was the frequency with which gay men changed sexual partners.

Violence), for de facto bans on private ownership and use of virtually all arms.

[118] Approximately 40% of all reported AIDS cases in 1986 were from either New York City or San Francisco. Peter S. Arno and Robert G. Hughes, *Local Policy Responses to the AIDS Epidemic: New York and San Francisco*, in ACQUIRED IMMUNODEFICIENCY SYNDROME 11-19 (Pascal James Imperato Jr. MD ed.) (1989).

One of the principal correlations between multiple partners and AIDS was the prevalence of anonymous and uninhibited sexual conduct at gay bathhouses. As a result, gay bathhouses became a focus of the efforts to curb the AIDS epidemic.[119]

In early 1984, San Francisco's Department of Public Health ordered the closure of all gay bathhouses in the city, citing the AIDS epidemic as justification for taking this action.[120] Shortly thereafter, a number of bathhouses

---

[119] Stephen L. Collier, *Preventing the Spread of AIDS by Restricting Sexual Conduct in Gay Bathhouses: A Constitutional Analyses,* 15 GOLDEN. GATE U.. L. REV. 301, 313-329 (1985) (chronicling the history of AIDS and the role homosexual sexual activity in bathhouses played in the spread of the disease and concluding that any law that regulated sexual activity for public health purposes would have to survive a strict scrutiny review, which would "prevent the use of a bathhouse sex limitation as precedent for further restrictions on gay sexual activity.")

[120] *The AIDS Epidemic in San Francisco: The Medical Response. 1981-1984. Volume I, an oral history conducted 1992-1993*, THE BANCROFT LIBRARY, UNIVERSITY OF CALIFORNIA, BERKELEY, 1995 (hereinafter, the "Oral History"), at page 91 (available at

defied the closure order and Dr. Mervyn Silverman, the director of the Department of Public Health, sought and received a temporary restraining order from the California Superior Court closing the city's bathhouses.[121]

That order was subsequently lifted by the California Superior Court a month later, allowing gay bathhouses to reopen so long as they complied with enumerated AIDS prevention measures.[122]

---

http://archive.org/stream/aidsepidemicinsf01chinrich/aidsepidemicinsf01chinrich_djvu.txt).

[121] *Oral History, supra* note 120.

[122] *Id.* at 254. The revised order allowed for bathhouses to reopen subject to the following conditions "1) no private rooms can be rented unless they are licensed to be operated as hotel rooms; (2) employees of the establishment shall be assigned to observe the activity on the premises, the number of monitors needed is specified in the court order. They shall survey the entire premises every ten minutes and expel all patrons observed in high risk sexual activity as defined by the Health Department. Owners must report to the Health Department on the number of people expelled; (3) all doors to individual cubicles or booths must be removed; (4) owners shall educate patrons on what

Though it was widely believed that San Francisco had permanently closed the city's gay bathhouses, from and after the date of the lifting of the order gay bathhouses have been allowed to operate in San Francisco, subject to requirements promulgated by San Francisco's Department of Public Health that are substantially similar to the conditions outlined in the Superior Court's order.[123] The AIDS crisis and the perceived high risk of disease transmissions at the bathhouses, however, resulted in such public trepidation that many of the bathhouses closed due to lack of patronage.[124]

---

constitutes high risk sexual activity; and (5) if violations of the court order are found by the Health Department, the owner shall be given 5 days from written notice to cure the violation. After that, the Health Department can close the facility."

[123] *See* Evelyn Nieves, *San Francisco Again Debates Over Bathhouses,"* N.Y. TIMES (May 29, 1999), available at http://partners.nytimes.com/library/national/science/aids/052999aids-frisco-baths.html.

[124] *Id.*

In recent years, however, there have been numerous calls for the termination of AIDS prevention measures that have been imposed on bathhouses.[125] Prominent San Francisco activists and political leaders have argued that the measures

> ...[don't] have a basis in public health and [are] arbitrary. Gay men have various ways of meeting other gay men for sex, whether in bars, bathhouses, or online. To claim, as this rule does, that having sex in a private room in a bathhouse is somehow riskier than going to someone's house or having public sex in a bathhouse, makes no

---

[125] *Id. See, also,* Seth Hemmelgarn, *City Ponders Bathhouse Rules,* THE BAY AREA REPORTER (August 8, 2013), available at http://www.ebar.com/news/article.php?sec=news&article=68989.

sense....[126]

It should be noted at this point that other than for a few months in 1984, there never was a ban on gay bathhouses in San Francisco and no California court had ever ruled on the legality of the closures while they were in effect.

A year later, New York State did in fact authorize local officials to close any facilities "in which high risk sexual activity takes place," deeming such facilities public nuisances dangerous to the public health.[127] This law was upheld by the New York Supreme Court, ruling that the AIDS epidemic justified the potential infringement of

---

[126] *Statement of San Francisco City Supervisor Scott Wiener*, representing the city's Castro district, a neighborhood with a prominent gay community. *Id.*

[127] *See* New York v. New St. Mark's Baths, 130 Misc.2d 911, 913 (1986) (citing through State Sanitary Code (10 NYCRR) § 24.2).

individual rights.[128]

What makes the New York bathhouse closures significant is the fact that they were not a blanket order for all bathhouses to cease operations. Rather, local authorities had to observe patrons engaging in high risk sexual activity in particular bathhouse and then seek a closure order for a specified duration of time, applicable only to that bathhouse. There were several high profile bathhouse closures, but ultimately the city's authority to close bathhouses was infrequently used and, like in San Francisco, public fear over the spread of AIDS led to significant declines in patronage of New York City bathhouses. Remaining bathhouse patrons began regulating their own behavior to avoid unsafe sexual

---

[128] Id. at 916, with a permanent injunction issued at 168 A.D.2d 311, 562 N.Y.S.2d 642 (N.Y. App. Div. 1st Dep't 1990).

practices that were likely lead to the spread of AIDS.[129]

New York City's response to the AIDS epidemic was the most draconian of all major United States' cities; others such as Los Angeles, did not attempt to close gay bathhouses and resorted to public education campaigns to encourage safe sex practices.[130]

In sum, even though the AIDS epidemic resulted in hundreds of thousands of deaths in the United States, there were never restrictions on private conduct and the only bans that were upheld were those affecting specifically identified individual commercial enterprises that had been found to be in violation of public health laws. As a note, if arms were regulated in a corresponding manner, criminals would be subject to bans but there would be no

---

[129] *See* Scott Bronstein, *4 New York Bathhouses Remain Still Operate Under City's Program of Inspections* N.Y. TIMES (May 3, 1987).

[130] *Nieves*, supra note 123.

presumption that gun owners were criminals who should be deprived of a basic right.

(4) "Stop and Frisk" Police Practices under the Fourth Amendment.

In a recent decision from the Southern District of New York (the "SDNY Opinion"),[131] the police practice of stopping and frisking individuals (the "Stop and Frisk

---

[131] The opinion in this case was in two parts. The first opinion dealt with the court's conclusions of law: See *Floyd v. City of New York*, --- F. Supp. 2d ----, No. 08 Civ. 1034, 2013 WL 4046209 (S.D.N.Y. Aug. 12, 2013) (hereinafter "Liability Op."); the second opinion dealt with the court's remedies: See *Floyd v. City of New York*, --- F. Supp. 2d ----, Nos. 08 Civ, 1034, 12 Civ. 2274, 2013 WL 4046217 (S.D.N.Y. Aug. 12, 2013) (hereinafter "Remedies Op.") The Remedies Op is not relevant for the analysis of this case. Subsequent to the publication of the Liability Op the Second Circuit stayed the decision, including the matters described in the Remedies Op. As of the date of this paper the City of New York and the plaintiffs are negotiating a settlement in lieu of further court proceedings.

Policy") [132] was found to violate the Fourth Amendment.[133] From the outset of the Liability Opinion the court was remarkably clear in announcing a fundamental premise:

---

[132] The Liability Op. set forth the legal standards for police stops:

> The Fourth Amendment protects all individuals against unreasonable searches or seizures. The Supreme Court has held that the Fourth Amendment permits the police to "stop and briefly detain a person for investigative purposes if the officer has a reasonable suspicion supported by articulable facts that criminal activity 'may be afoot,' even if the officer lacks probable cause." "Reasonable suspicion is an objective standard; hence, the subjective intentions or motives of the officer making the stop are irrelevant." The test for whether a stop has taken place in the context of a police encounter is whether a reasonable person would have felt free to terminate the encounter. "'[T]o proceed from a stop to a frisk, the police officer must reasonably suspect that the person stopped is armed and dangerous." Liability Op. at 5 (citations omitted).

[133] *Liability Op., supra* note 132, at 13. The "stop and frisk" policy was also found to be a violation of the Fourteenth Amendment, but for purposes of this paper the Fourth Amendment findings are most illustrative and thus will be the focus of this section.

"… this case is not about the effectiveness of stop and frisk in deterring or combating crime. This Court's mandate is solely to judge the constitutionality of police behavior, not its effectiveness as a law enforcement tool. Many police practices may be useful for fighting crime — preventive detention or coerced confessions, for example — but because they are unconstitutional they cannot be used, no matter how effective."[134]

New York City's Stop and Frisk Policy was first instituted as a means to prevent violent crime by targeting those individuals that the police believed fit a certain profile for stops based on "a reasonable suspicion that criminal activity may be afoot"[135] From there, a frisk for weapons could be conducted if the officer "reasonably

---

[134] *Id.* at 2.

[135] *Id.* at 22.

believes that the person stopped is armed and dangerous."[136]

Under the Stop and Frisk Policy, the basis for each stop had to be recorded by the officer conducting the investigation and the New York City Police Department maintained a database of all of these reports. The stopping officer was required to complete and file a form that indicated the basis for each stop by marking a box with the general description of the reason for the stop, such as "furtive movements", "high crime area".[137] It should be noted that even though each police officer was required to complete a form for each stop, the court found that the database was "highly flawed" due to the subjective nature of the forms and the fact that it was not possible to know

---

[136] *Id.* at 24.

[137] *Id.* at 8. Furtive movements was the basis for 42% of all recorded stops and high crime area was the basis for 55% of all recorded stops. *Id.*

whether a form was properly completed and filed for each stop.[138]

Based on these data, it was shown that between 2004 and 2012 there were over 4.4 million stop incidents, resulting in approximately 2.3 million frisk incidents, with weapons being found in less than 2% of all frisks.[139] After reviewing expert testimony on the data the court found that at least 6% of all stops were without reasonable suspicion and concluded that this violated the Fourth Amendment in that "…that relatively small *percentage* still represents 200,000 individuals who were stopped without reasonable suspicion. Even this number of wrongful stops produces a significant human toll."[140]

---

[138] Compare this to the absolute reliance of the Sunnyvale and San Francisco Courts on a database that was far more subjective and far less complete. See *supra* note 25 and accompanying text.

[139] *Liability Op., supra* note 132. at 32.

[140] Id. at 41. The standard of scrutiny for Fourth Amendment cases is somewhat unique in that a search must be based on reasonable

Like the Magazine Bans, the Stop and Frisk Policy was instituted to fight crime and promote public safety. The SDNY Opinion did not dispute the fact that for these purposes, the Stop and Frisk Policy, like the gang assembly ban in *Morales*, was successful in preventing crime. Indeed, all indications were that the Stop and Frisk Policy played a significant role in the dramatic decrease in crime in New York City, to the point that New York City had become the safest big city in America at the time of the case.[141]

---

suspicion. As a result, the comparison to strict or intermediate scrutiny is not directly applicable. Arguably, reasonable suspicion is most closely related to rational basis scrutiny. This is obviously a simplification of Fourth Amendment standards. For a more complete discussion, see THOMAS N. MCINNIS, THE EVOLUTION OF THE FOURTH AMENDMENT (2009).

[141] Citing to the City of New York's Statement of Facts, the court earlier had noted that "...in 1995, murder rates decreased 33.9 percent from the previous year, from 1,181 to 1,582; that in 2009, there were 471 murders, the lowest level since 1964; and that since 2003, crime has

Nonetheless, the SDNY Opinion stated that the effectiveness of the policy was not relevant in determining its constitutionality.[142] What did matter, however, was the *frequency* with which the Stop and Frisk Policy resulted in the infringement of innocent citizens' Fourth Amendment rights.

---

dropped approximately 76 percent." Floyd v. City of New York, 813 F. Supp. 2d 417 (S.D.N.Y. 2011) at note 6. *See, also*, Brad Hamilton, *NYC On Track To Be Nations' Safest* City, N.Y. POST, Nov. 2., 2013, available at http://nypost.com/2013/11/02/nyc-on-track-to-be-nations-safest-city/ ("Murder in New York has dropped to levels not seen since the 1950s, and is falling so fast the Big Apple could finish the year with the lowest homicide rate of any big city in the nation. There have been 279 homicides in the city through Oct. 31, down 23 percent from the 364 logged in the same 10-month period last year. The city is on pace for about 100 fewer slayings this year than the 419 it recorded last year, which was the lowest figure since 1962 when police began keeping reliable records. If the current average of less than one homicide a day holds, New York would see 334 killings by year's end. Police officials believe homicides haven't been that low since 1956 and 1957. The all-time high was 2,245 in 1990.")

[142] *Liability Op., supra* note 132, at 2.

A 6% infringement rate was considered to be a violation of the Fourth Amendment.[143]

iv) Comparative Public Safety Data

In the cases discussed in Section III hereof the common justification for laws that restricted constitutional rights was public safety. It is therefore important to dig deeper into the data behind the public safety concerns for those laws to determine how the Magazine Bans compare to laws that have not survived constitutional scrutiny.

The Magazine Bans were justified as a response to several high profile mass casualty shooting incidents over

---

[143] The Magazine Bans have an effective infringement rate of 100%, as they constitute an absolute ban on a Second Amendment right.

the course of the previous six years. To wit, San Francisco Police Code § 619 (hereinafter, "Section 619"), where the San Francisco Magazine Ban is codified, includes in its findings the following:

Large capacity magazines were used in a number of recent high-profile shootings, including:

- *The shooting on the campus of Virginia Tech on April 16, 2007, where 32 people were killed and many others wounded,*
- *The shooting in a gym in Pittsburgh on August 4, 2009, where three people were killed and nine others injured.*
- *The shooting on November 5, 2009 at Fort Hood, Texas, where 13*

> *people were killed and 34 more were wounded.*
>
> - *The shooting on January 8, 2011, at Tucson, Arizona, where 6 people were killed and 13 people were injured, including a member of the United States House of Representatives, and*
>
> - *The shootings on December 14, 2012, at Newtown, Connecticut, where 27 people (not including the shooter) were killed.*[144]

Perhaps because none of the cited "high-profile shootings" occurred in San Francisco, let alone California, Section 619 includes in its findings the statement that "[i]n 2007, 3,231 people died from firearm-related injuries in

---

[144] San Francisco Police Code §619(a)(6).

California."[145]

San Francisco provided no source for this data, but according to the Federal Bureau of Investigation there were a total of 2,249 murders in California in 2007, with 1,605 of these being firearms-related murders.[146] A recent Pew Research study found that suicides constitute over 60% of all reported firearms related deaths,[147] which roughly corresponds with the premise that San Francisco included suicide-by-firearm data in its Section 619 finding.

---

[145] San Francisco Police Code §619(a)(1). There was no source provided for this data.

[146] U.S. DEP'T OF JUSTICE, FEDERAL BUREAU OF INVESTIGATION, UNIFORM CRIME REPORTS, MURDER BY STATE, TYPE OF WEAPON 2007 TABLE 20, available at http://www.fbi.gov/about-us/cjis/ucr/crime-in-the-u.s/2007.

[147] D'Vera Cohn, Paul Taylor, Mark Hugo Lopez, Catherine A. Gallagher, Kim Parker and Kevin T. Maass, *Gun Homicide Rate Down 49% Since 1993 Peak; Public Unaware*, PEW RESEARCH SOCIAL & DEMOGRAPHIC TRENDS, May 7, 2013 (hereinafter, the "Pew Gun Report"), available at http://www.pewsocialtrends.org/files/2013/05/firearms_final_05-2013.pdf.

Section 619 was not promoted as a suicide prevention measure, so the fact that the sponsors of the legislation included data, a majority of which were irrelevant to the goal of preventing "high-profile shootings," is mysterious, at best, and certainly sounds like a case of the government not "pursuing the interest it invokes" as justification for a law.[148] It is among the truest of truisms that it is a rare suicide where more than 10 rounds of ammunition are fired.

In fact, there have been no recent mass shootings in either San Francisco or Sunnyvale and since "large capacity magazines" are generally not permitted for sale or transfer in California, the odds that any of the cited 3,231 firearms-related deaths were caused by the availability or use of such magazines are minute. Neither San Francisco nor

---

[148] *Brown, supra* note 100.

Sunnyvale provided any data to support the claim that "large capacity magazines" constituted "an actual problem in need of solving" (if we were to apply the standard set out in *Brown*) in either city.

Furthermore, though both cities pointed to several high-profile mass shootings, the CRS Report demonstrates that such shootings are exceedingly rare in the United States[149] and the Pew Gun Report shows that in 2010 (the most recent year for which final data are available) "[t]he [national] gun homicide rate… was the lowest it had been since CDC began publishing data in 1981."[150]

As an example of how local government agencies and their aligned interest groups distort firearms-related death data, a recent report by the Law Center to Prevent

---

[149] *See* CRS Report, *supra* note 40.

[150] Pew Gun Report, *supra* note 147, at 11.

Gun Violence is illustrative.[151] The LC Report stated that "[i]n 1993, 5,500 Californians were killed by gunfire; by 2010, the most recent year for which data is available, that number had dropped to 2,935."[152] The problem with this claim is both the 5,500 and the 2,935 numbers include firearms-related deaths due to suicides, accidents and law enforcement activity. Suicide-by-firearm alone for 2010 constituted 1,492 of the 2,935 firearms-related deaths. The actual number of homicides involving firearms in 2010 was 1,342, which includes cases of self defense as well as cases of violent offensive assault.[153] More than half of the deaths reported in the LC report were therefore misleadingly

---

[151] LAW CENTER TO PREVENT GUN VIOLENCE, The *California Model: Twenty Years of Putting Safety First*, dated June 18, 2013 (hereinafter, the "LC Report"), available at http://smartgunlaws.org/wp-content/uploads/2013/07/20YearsofSuccess_ForWebFINAL3.pdf.

[152] *Id.* at page titled "Proof in the Data".

[153] Data obtained at the Centers for Disease Control Fatal Injury database, available at http://webappa.cdc.gov/sasweb/ncipc/dataRestriction_inj.html.

characterized in order to overstate the actual risks of firearms. Since homicides are the principal result of the type of firearms misuse that laws like the Magazine Bans are intended to prevent, it is this figure that should be the focus of analysis.

I would like to highlight the 1,342 number as yardstick for the analysis that follows. Clearly, very few of the 1,342 firearms-related homicides in California in 2010 involved "large capacity magazines": no data on this subject were reported in either District Court Order and since the sale of such magazines has been prohibited in California for decades, it is unlikely that even a small percentage of firearms-related homicides in California involve them. But for purposes of the following analysis in this paper, I will use the data provided as part of the

Sunnyvale Order to assume that 17%[154] of the 1,342 firearms-related homicides in California in 2010 involved "large capacity magazines" and none of these cases were

---

[154] The 17% rate was noted in a declaration filed by Professor Christopher Koper in support of the Sunnyvale Magazine Ban. Professor Koper stated that he found that "...guns linked to murders were 8% to 17% more likely to have ["large capacity magazines"] than guns linked to non-fatal gunshot victimizations..." in one of his studies. I will use Professor Koper's high-end estimate, which is likely magnitudes greater than the actual percent for California since California has already banned the sale and transfer of "large capacity magazines", while the area in Professor Koper's study had no such restrictions. *See* Declaration of Professor Christopher Koper (hereinafter, the "Koper Declaration"), ¶24, available at http://michellawyers.com/wp-content/uploads/2013/12/Fyock-v.-Sunnyvale_Declaration-of-Christopher-S.-Koper-In-Support-of-Sunnyvales-Opposition-to-Plaintiffs-Motion-for-Preliminary-Injunction.pdf. The 17% figure is further bolstered by ¶16 of the Koper Declaration: "Prior to the federal assault weapons ban, for example, guns with [large capacity magazines] were used in roughly 13-26% of most gun crimes." 17% is the midpoint between 13% and 26%, and if the use of "large capacity magazines" in homicides tracks their use in gun crime generally, the 17% should represent an accurate estimate of the percentage of firearms homicides involving "large capacity magazines".

self defense.

Using these assumptions, there were an estimated 228 firearms-related homicides in California in 2010 that involved "large capacity magazines". We are told that this justifies the infringement of an enumerated constitutional right.

How do the estimated 228 "large capacity magazine" homicides compare to other causes of death in California in 2010?

According to the California Department of Public Health[155] there were 233,143 total deaths in California in

---

[155] STATE OF CALIFORNIA, DEPARTMENT OF PUBLIC HEALTH, DEATH RECORDS, Table 5-8, *Thirteen Leading Causes of Death by Race/Ethnic Group and Sex, California,* 2010, available at http://www.cdph.ca.gov/data/statistics/Documents/VSC-2010-0508.pdf.

2010. The top 13 causes of death were as follows[156]:

---

[156] *Id.*

Cause of Death	Number of Deaths
Diseases of the Heart	58,034
Malignant Neoplasms	56,124
Cerebrovascular Diseases	13,566
Chronic Lower Respiratory Disease	12,928
Alzheimer's Disease	10,833
Accidents	10,108
Diabetes Mellitus	7,027
Influenza and Pneumonia	5,856
Chronic Liver Disease and Cirrhosis	4,252
Intentional Self Harm	3,835
Essential Hypertension/Hypertensive Renal Disease	3,722
Nephritis	3,073
Parkinson's Disease	2,232

Though it was not in the top 13 causes of death, homicides (including non-firearms related homicides) for 2010 in California totaled 1,809.[157] It is clear that the estimated 228 homicides involving "large capacity magazines", representing only 12% of all homicides and approximately .001% of all deaths in California for 2010, were a statistically insignificant cause of death by any measure.

The number of deaths attributable to AIDS in California in 2010, however, at 1,627,[158] was over 700% greater than the 228 fatalities estimated to be attributable to

---

[157] CALIFORNIA DEPARTMENT OF JUSTICE, CALIFORNIA HOMICIDE STATISTICS FOR 2010 at table 1, available at
http://ag.ca.gov/cms_attachments/press/pdfs/n2587_homicide_in_ca_2010_.pdf

[158] THE HENRY J. KAISER FAMILY FOUNDATION STATE HEALTH FACTS, ESTIMATED DEATHS OF ADULTS AND ADOLESCENTS WITH AN HIV DIAGNOSIS, 2010 (hereinafter, the "KFF 2010 Report"), available at
http://kff.org/hivaids/state-indicator/estimated-deaths-of-adults-and-adolescents-with-an-hiv-diagnosis/.

homicides involving "large capacity magazines" for the same period.

Extending the analysis to a national level, there were 19,338[159] deaths attributable to AIDS in the United States in 2010 compared to an estimated 1,883 homicides involving "large capacity magazines".[160]

---

[159] *Id.*

[160] Sherry L. Murphy, B.S.; Jiaquan Xu, M.D.; and Kenneth D. Kochanek, M.A., U.S DEP'T OF HEALTH AND HUMAN SERVICES, CENTERS FOR DISEASE CONTROL, *Deaths, Final Data for 2010* in National Vital Statistics Report, Vol. 61, No. 4, Table 10 (hereinafter, the "2010 CDC Report"), available at http://www.cdc.gov/nchs/data/nvsr/nvsr61/nvsr61_04.pdf. For further reference, there were a total of 2,468,435 deaths from all causes in the United States in 2010. Id. The estimate of 1,883 "large capacity magazine" related homicides was arrived at by applying the 17% derived from the study referenced in note 154 hereof to the 11,078 firearms-related homicides for 2010. As with the use of this percentage to estimate California's "large capacity magazine" related homicides, this likely over-estimates the number of deaths related to "large capacity magazines" since such magazines were subject to bans in other states in 2010 (*see* http://www.handgunlaw.us/documents/NoHiCapChemSpray.pdf), but

The death rate from AIDS has dropped precipitously over the past 30 years as a result of education, the proliferation of safe sex practices and new drug therapies, all measures that did not involve the prohibition of any sexual practice or the permanent closure or banning of any public venue in which high risk sexual practices typically.[161] Nonetheless, the cumulative number of AIDS related deaths in the United States was over 636,000 at 2010,[162] with over 95,000 of those fatalities having been in

---

since the CDC data are not parsed beyond the general classification of firearms-related homicides it is not possible to obtain more specific data.

[161] THE HENRY J. KAISER FAMILY FOUNDATION, *The HIV/AUDS Epidemic in the United States,* published Mar. 22, 2013 (hereinafter, the "KFF Epidemic Report"), available at http://kff.org/hivaids/fact-sheet/the-hivaids-epidemic-in-the-united-states/. *See, also,* CENTERS FOR DISEASE CONTROL AND PREVENTION. *HIV Surveillance Report, 2011;* vol. 23 at Table 12a, published February 2013, available at http://www.cdc.gov/hiv/pdf/statistics_2011_HIV_Surveillance_Report_vol_23.pdf.

[162] *Id.*

California.[163] Overall, "California ranks second in the nation in cumulative AIDS cases at 157,719"[164] and according to the AIDS Informational Website, homosexual and bisexual men account for over 60% of new HIV infections.[165] While the percentages have varied over time, there is no question that AIDS is a deadly disease primarily affecting homosexuals and spread in large part by

---

[163] STATE OF CALIFORNIA, DEPARTMENT OF PUBLIC HEALTH, OFFICE OF AIDS, HIV/AIDS SURVEILLANCE SECTION, *December 2013 Semi-annual Surveillance Report, Table 1*, (hereinafter, the "2013 CA AIDS Report") available at http://www.cdph.ca.gov/programs/aids/Documents/Dec_2013_Semi_Annual%20Report.pdf.

[164] SAN FRANCISCO AIDS FOUNDATION, *Statistics* (hereinafter "SF AIDS Website"), available at http://www.sfaf.org/hiv-info/statistics/.

[165] AIDS Informational Website, *supra* note 114, at *U.S. Statistics* (available at http://aids.gov/hiv-aids-basics/hiv-aids-101/statistics/#ref2) ("Although [Gay, bisexual, and other men who have sex with men] represent about 4% of the male population in the United States4, in 2010, MSM accounted for 78% of new HIV infections among males and 63% of all new infections").

homosexual sexual activity.[166]

In the same period nationally, there were 40,393 drug-induced deaths, 35,332 motor vehicle accident related deaths, 26,009 deaths from falls, 25,692 alcohol-induced deaths, 3,782 accidental drowning related deaths and 2,490 deaths resulting from complications of medical care.[167]

---

[166] Id. "Gay, bisexual, and other men who have sex with men (MSM) of all races and ethnicities remain the population most profoundly affected by HIV". See, also, CENTERS FOR DISEASE CONTROL AND PREVENTION. *HIV Among Gay, Bisexual and Other Men Who Have Sex with Men*, Fact Sheet published Sept. 26, 2013, available at http://www.cdc.gov/hiv/risk/gender/msm/facts/index.html ("Sexual risk behaviors account for most HIV infections in [Gay, bisexual, and other men who have sex with men]. Anal sex without a condom (unprotected anal sex) has the highest risk for passing HIV during sex. It is also possible to become infected with HIV through oral sex, though the risk is significantly less than for anal or vaginal sex. For sexually active [Gay, bisexual, and other men who have sex with men], the most effective ways to prevent HIV are to limit or avoid anal sex, or for [Gay, bisexual, and other men who have sex with men]who do have anal sex, to correctly use a condom every time.")

[167] 2010 CDC Report, *supra* note 160.

The cause of death that was closest in number to the estimated homicides from "large capacity magazines" was hernias, with 1,832 deaths in 2010.[168] The author of this paper is unaware, after diligent inquiry, of any law that purports to protect the public from hernia-related fatalities.

Since both District Court Orders were based either explicitly or implicitly[169] on the goal of preventing mass shooting events, it's useful to examine other fatality incidents that have similar characteristics to mass shootings (hereinafter, "Mass Casualty Events"); to wit, an indiscriminate single public event with a death count of at least four. Given that the District Court Orders referenced

---

[168] Id.

[169] The San Francisco Order explicitly stated that the San Francisco Magazine Ban was in response to mass shootings (*see, e.g.,* the San Francisco Order at 11) while the Sunnyvale Order was less explicit, though it still referenced mass shootings in justifying its ban (*see* the Sunnyvale Order at 14).

mass shootings occurring from 2007 through the date of each respective order, the following analysis will focus on Mass Casualty Events for the same timeframe.

Perhaps the most frequently occurring Mass Casualty Events in the United States are motor vehicle related fatalities. Since 2007, the following Mass Casualty Events involved large capacity vehicles[170]

- On April 10, 2014, 10 people were killed in California when a truck crossed into oncoming traffic and collided with a bus;[171]

---

[170] Descriptions of the following incidents appear at the National Transportation Safety Board's website. Links to the respective NTSB reports are provided for each incident. A large capacity vehicle is a truck, bus or train. It is not coincidental that I refer to these vehicles with the same general nomenclature as is used by anti-gun groups in describing the firearms that they seek to ban.

[171] http://www.sfgate.com/news/us/article/College-visit-turns-tragic-for-Calif-students-5394356.php

- On January 30, 2009, seven passengers were killed in Arizona when a bus rolled over after the driver lost control of the vehicle;[172]
- On February 15, 2014, four people were killed when a bus collided with a passenger car in Louisiana;[173]
- On November 15, 2012, a train collided with a truck in Texas, killing four people;[174]
- On June 24, 2011, a train collided with a truck in Nevada, killing six people;[175]
- On May 31, 2011, the driver of a bus in Virginia lost control of the vehicle, resulting in four deaths;[176]

---

[172] https://www.ntsb.gov/investigations/summary/HAR1001.html

[173] https://www.ntsb.gov/doclib/reports/2014/HWY14MH006_Centerville_LA_PreliminaryReport.pdf

[174] https://www.ntsb.gov/investigations/summary/HAR1302.html

[175] https://www.ntsb.gov/investigations/summary/HAR1203.html

[176] https://www.ntsb.gov/investigations/summary/HAR1202.html

- On March 12, 2011, the driver of a bus lost control of the vehicle in New York, resulting in 15 deaths;[177]
- On March 26, 2010, a truck collided with a van in Kentucky, killing 11 people;[178]
- On August 8, 2008, a bus ran off a roadway in Texas, killing 17 people;[179]
- On January 6, 2008, a the driver of a bus in Utah lost control of the vehicle, killing nine people;[180]
- On August 1, 2007, 111 vehicles were on a bridge in Minnesota when the bridge failed, resulting in 13 fatalities;[181]
- On March 2, 2007, a bus ran off the

---

[177] https://www.ntsb.gov/investigations/summary/HAR1201.html
[178] https://www.ntsb.gov/investigations/summary/HAR1102.html
[179] https://www.ntsb.gov/investigations/summary/HAR0902.htm
[180] https://www.ntsb.gov/investigations/summary/HAR0901.htm
[181] https://www.ntsb.gov/investigations/summary/HAR0803.htm

roadway in Georgia, killing seven people;[182]

- On December 1, 2013, a commuter train in New York derailed, killing four people;[183]

- On September 12, 2008, a freight train and a commuter train collided in California, killing 25 people;[184] and

- On December 30, 2012, 9 people were killed in Oregon when a tour bus went off the roadway.[185]

While data are not available for casualties per incident relating specifically to large capacity vehicles used by schools to transport children, according to the National Highway Transportation Safety Administration, since 2002

---

[182] https://www.ntsb.gov/investigations/summary/HAR0801.htm
[183] https://www.ntsb.gov/doclib/reports/2014/Metro-North_Bronx%202013_PreliminaryReport.pdf
[184] https://www.ntsb.gov/investigations/summary/RAR1001.html
[185] http://www.cnn.com/2012/12/30/us/oregon-bus-crash/

there has been an average of 135 fatalities per year involving school buses of all sizes and types.[186] Compare this to the average of 18 fatalities per year from mass shootings.[187] If protecting the lives of children was the basis for the Magazine Bans (and the legislative finding references therein to the Columbine and Sandy Hook tragedies clearly indicate that this was the case), school buses should have been banned years ago.

When it comes to passenger vehicles (i.e., cars and trucks used for passengers, not including large capacity buses and trains) the data are no less grim. The following are a sample of Mass Casualty Events involving passenger vehicles since 2009 (this data should be reviewed with

---

[186] U.S. DEP'T OF TRANSPORTATION, NATIONAL HIGHWAY TRANSPORTATION SAFETY ADMINISTRATION, *Traffic Safety Facts 2002-2011* (June 2013) DOT HS 811 746, available at http://www-nrd.nhtsa.dot.gov/Pubs/811746.pdf.

[187] CRS Report, *supra* note 40.

understanding that it is not only a sample, rather than an all-inclusive listing, it is also for a period that is approximately 25% shorter than the corresponding Mass Shooting data, which goes back to 2007).

- On September 18, 2010, six people were killed when a the tire of a van in New York failed, resulting in a rollover crash;[188]
- On May 20, 2013, five people were killed in Illinois when a van rolled over;[189]
- On March 7, 2014, four people were killed when a car and a pickup truck collided in Minnesota;[190]

---

[188] http://www.recordonline.com/apps/pbcs.dll/article?AID=/20100919/NEWS/9190325

[189] http://www.stltoday.com/news/local/crime-and-courts/five-dead-six-injured-in-crash-of--passenger-van/article_d38efefc-fcfc-5c35-b69c-13649e779bdf.html

[190] http://www.startribune.com/local/249099551.html

- On July 22, 2012, 14 people were killed when a pickup truck driver in Texas lost control of the vehicle and collided with several trees;[191]
- On February 9, 2014, in two separate incidents, a total of 11 people were killed in car accidents in Florida and California;[192]
- On July 26, 2009, eight people were killed in New York when an SUV collided with a minivan;[193]
- On May 3, 2014, four people were killed in a three vehicle incident in Missouri;[194]
- On March 29, 2014, five people were killed

---

[191] http://news.yahoo.com/blogs/lookout/pickup-truck-crash-texas-photo-144056003.html

[192] http://www.latimes.com/nation/nationnow/la-na-nn-wrong-way-crash-florida-20140210,0,3557331.story#axzz2xm6w8SRK

[193] http://www.nytimes.com/2009/08/03/nyregion/03crash.html

[194] http://www.ozarksfirst.com/story/d/story/four-killed-in-newton-county-crash-two-from-sprin/63553/t9NtlYxCGkK9WfKS8gakzg

in Arizona when a truck collided with a semi-trailer truck.[195]

- On January 29, 2012, 10 people were killed in a chain collision accident in Florida;[196]
- On March 13, 2014, a car was driven into a crowd of people in Texas, killing four;[197]
- On February 9, 2014, five people were killed in Florida in a collision between a car and an SUV;[198]
- On May 1, 2014, six people were killed in

---

[195] http://www.azcentral.com/story/news/local/pinal/2014/03/30/truck-collision-interstate-freeway-deaths-family/7077569/

[196] http://www.cbsnews.com/news/i-75-crash-one-georgia-churchs-tragedy/

[197] http://www.huffingtonpost.com/2014/03/27/sxsw-crash-death_n_5044750.html

[198] http://www.wfla.com/story/24674285/five-killed-in-wrong-way-crash-on-i-275

Washington in four car collisions;[199]

- On October 2, 2013, eight people were killed when an SUV was hit by a bus in Tennessee;[200]
- On April 26, 2014, four people were killed in a wrong-way crash in Texas;[201]
- On April 29, 2012, seven people were killed when a van went off an elevated roadway in New York;[202]
- On April 4, 2014, four people were killed in New York when a car overturned on a

---

[199] http://www.kxly.com/news/spokane-news/six-killed-in-four-crashes-across-inland-northwest/25769684

[200] http://www.cnn.com/2013/10/02/us/tennessee-wreck/

[201] http://www.dallasnews.com/news/metro/20140426-wise-county-justice-of-peace-3-others-killed-in-crash.ece

[202] http://abclocal.go.com/wabc/story?section=news/local/new_york&id=8640845

roadway;[203]

- On May 29, 2013, seven people were killed when a minivan was hit by a semi-trailer truck in New York;[204]
- On May 10, 2014, five teenagers were killed when a car and an SUV collided in New York;[205]
- On May 11, 2014, five people were killed when a van and a car collided in California;[206]
- On April 16, 2014, four people were killed

---

[203] http://www.huffingtonpost.com/2014/04/05/car-flips-into-nyc-creek_n_5096476.html?1396703723&icid=maing-grid7%7Cmain5%7Cdl4%7Csec1_lnk2%26pLid%3D461555

[204] http://www.foxnews.com/us/2013/05/30/7-killed-in-crash-involving-tractor-trailer-and-minivan-in-upstate-new-york/

[205] http://www.nydailynews.com/new-york/family-friends-grieve-teens-killed-long-island-car-accident-article-1.1788575

[206] http://www.sfgate.com/news/us/article/5-killed-when-van-smashes-into-car-in-California-5470003.php

in a two car collision in Pennsylvania;[207] and

- On October 18, 2013, six people were killed in a collision between a car and a police cruiser in Ohio.[208]

Though this is not a complete listing of all Mass Casualty Events involving passenger vehicles for the five year period, the sample shows that approximately 130 people were killed in this sample period alone.[209] Using the average number of fatalities from Mass Shootings of 18 for comparison, the 130 Mass Casualty Events involving

---

[207] http://www.post-gazette.com/local/north/2014/04/17/4-killed-in-two-vehicle-crash-in-Armstrong-County/stories/201404170244

[208] http://www.nbcnews.com/news/other/six-killed-columbus-ohio-police-car-crash-f8C11417172

[209] The sample of Mass Casualty Events involving passenger vehicles and other large capacity vehicles was obtained by doing a simple Google search. Thus, it clearly does not include all such Mass Casualty Events and, consequently, undercounts such fatalities when compared to the CRS Report, which is an exhaustive and, presumably, complete accounting of all Mass Shootings.

passenger vehicles exceeds the number of fatalities from Mass Shootings (estimated at 108 for the period starting in 2009). If we were to add in the sampled number of Mass Casualty Event fatalities from large capacity vehicles for the same period (approximately 60), the sample of vehicle-related Mass Casualty Events roughly doubles the number of fatalities over the actual number attributable to Mass Shootings.

If one were to compare the total number of motor vehicle-related fatalities to the total number of firearms-related fatalities, the data make it clear that whether it comes to mass casualty fatalities or all fatalities overall, motor vehicles are significantly more likely to be associated with fatalities. To wit, there were approximately 260 million motor vehicles in the United States in 2010[210]

---

[210] U.S. DEP'T OF TRANSPORTATION, NATIONAL HIGHWAY TRANSPORTATION SAFETY ADMINISTRATION, *Traffic Safety Facts: 2010 DATA*(June 2012) DOT

and approximately 35,000 deaths caused by those vehicles in 2010.[211] For the same period, there were approximately 300 million firearms in the United States[212] and approximately 11,000 firearms-related homicides.[213] In comparative terms, while .004% of all firearms were associated with a homicide, .013% of all motor vehicles were associated with a fatality. Put another way, the rate of firearms-related homicides was 36.7 per million firearms while the rate of motor vehicle-related fatalities was 134.6 per million motor vehicles. By any accounting, motor vehicles have a fatality rate many times greater than that of

---

HS 811 630, available at http://www-nrd.nhtsa.dot.gov/Pubs/811630.pdf.

[211] Id. The fatality data from this report differs by approximately 3,000 from the data in the 2010 CDC Report. It is not clear why this discrepancy exists, but the 2010 CDC Report is subject to greater scrutiny so its data on fatalities will be relied upon in this paper.

[212] William J. Krouse, *Gun Control Legislation* (Congressional Research Service Report RL32842) (November 14, 2012), available at http://www.fas.org/sgp/crs/misc/RL32842.pdf.

[213] 2010 CDC Report, *supra* note 160.

firearms.

Expanding beyond Mass Casualty Events, a recent study found that over 18% of all deaths of adults in the United States between 1986 and 2006 were associated with obesity.[214] Other studies by the Centers for Disease Control have estimated the number of deaths related to obesity in the United States at between 112,000 and 365,000 per year.[215] These data show that obesity is clearly a far greater national public health threat than either the average of 18 mass shooting fatalities per year[216] or even

---

[214] Ryan K. Masters, Eric N. Reither, Daniel A. Powers, Y. Claire Yang, Andrew E. Burger, and Bruce G. Link. The Impact of Obesity on US Mortality Levels: The Importance of Age and Cohort Factors in Population Estimates. American Journal of Public Health: October 2013, Vol. 103, No. 10, pp. 1895-1901.

[215] CENTERS FOR DISEASE CONTROL AND PREVENTION. *Frequently asked questions about calculating obesity-related risk,* available at http://www.cdc.gov/PDF/Frequently_Asked_Questions_About_Calculating_Obesity-Related_Risk.pdf.

[216] *See* CRS Report, *supra* note 40

the estimated 1,883 fatalities attributable to "large capacity magazines" generally. [217]

Then again, in 2010 there were approximately 800 deaths nationwide attributable to bicycle accidents.[218] To put a point on this data, more people died on bicycles in one year than were killed in 30 years worth of mass shootings.[219]

So we are left with the obvious question: Given the relative insignificance of both mass shootings and "large capacity magazine"- related homicides in California and the United States, compared to such other causes of death such as AIDS, motor vehicle accidents, obesity or even

---

[217] See *supra* note 160.

[218] CENTERS FOR DISEASE CONTROL AND PREVENTION, *Bicycle-Related Injuries*, published on May 28, 2013, available at http://www.cdc.gov/HomeandRecreationalSafety/Bicycle/index.html.

[219] See CRS Report, *supra* note 40.

hernias, how can serve as the basis for the infringement of an enumerated constitutional right?

v) The Nature of the Second Amendment Right Balanced Against Legitimate Government Interests.

At this point supporters of expansive government regulation of firearms will argue that many of the examples that have been used in the previous section of this paper are not relevant since deaths from, say, motor vehicles or obesity are a minor and acceptable consequence of the overwhelmingly beneficial uses of the underlying modalities. Moreover, supporters of government policies that infringe the Second Amendment often argue that the need to save innocent lives outweighs any Second Amendment interests.

The San Francisco Order contains a sterling example of this type of argument:

> *In assessing the balance of equities, those rare occasions [when a law-abiding citizen needs more than 10 rounds to defend himself] must be weighed against the more frequent and documented occasions when a mass murderer with a gun holding eleven or more rounds empties the magazine and slaughters innocents. One critical difference is that whereas the civilian defender rarely will exhaust the up-to-ten magazine, the mass murderer has every intention of firing every round possible and will exhaust the largest magazine available to him. On balance, more innocent lives will be saved by limiting the capacity of magazines than by allowing the previous regime of no*

limitation to continue.[220]

The San Francisco Order further pointed out that "...86 percent of mass shootings in the past 30 years involved at least one magazine that could hold more than 10 rounds..." and posited that "...more people are injured and killed per mass shooting with such magazines than without..." prior to concluding that "...San Francisco's interest in preventing another Sandy Hook tragedy constitutes a 'critical public interest.'"[221]

Being charitable, the San Francisco Court played fast, loose and disingenuous with its balance of equities analysis. As shown in the CRS Report, the average annual number of deaths related to mass shootings in the past 30 years was 18 across the entire nation. For the San Francisco

---

[220] San Francisco Order, *supra* note 2, at 11.
[221] *Id.*

Court to claim that this constitutes a "more frequent" occasion than a legal use of "large capacity magazines" is utterly without basis in logic, fact or reason.

As a preliminary matter, while the San Francisco Court used a national statistic on mass shootings on one side of its balance of equities analysis, it didn't use national statistics on the lawful use of "large capacity magazines" on the other side of its analysis. It simply reverted to a presumption that the lawful use of "large capacity magazines" was rare. One would have to have a database of all lawful uses of "large capacity magazines", as there is a database for the number of mass shootings, to have a meaningful analysis. Alas, no database exists to document the number of lawful uses of "large capacity magazines."

It takes more than a non-empirical conclusion (the claim by the San Francisco Court that the lawful use of "large capacity magazines" is rare) to conduct a balance of equities analysis.

In point of fact, though, the San Francisco Court engaged in a more significant analytical flaw: it limited its balance of equities analysis to self defense, while the Second Amendment is in no way limited to the protection of the right to keep and bear arms solely for self defense.

While the *Heller* court stated that one of the primary rights covered by the Second Amendment is "defense of hearth and home" it certainly didn't limit the Second Amendment right to self defense.

Historically, the right to keep and bear arms has been focused on hunting, as well as self defense and the *Heller* opinion clearly recognized this fact: "The prefatory clause [of the Second Amendment] does not suggest that preserving the militia was the only reason Americans valued the ancient right; most undoubtedly thought it even more important for self-defense and **hunting**."[222] *Heller* just happened to be a challenge to a law that infringed on the right to use a weapon commonly used for self defense, which is why the *Heller* decision focused on the self defense aspect of the Second Amendment. To ignore the equally important hunting aspects of the Second Amendment protections, however, is to ignore the entirety of the *Heller* court's explanation of the limitations the Second Amendment placed upon the government's ability to regulate arms and the corresponding inherent right of the people to keep and bear arms for hunting purposes.

As Justice Scalia wrote in *Heller*, "…the Second Amendment was not intended to lay down a novel principle but rather codified a right inherited from our English

---

[222] *Heller*, slip op. at 26 (emphasis added).

ancestors."[223] That is, the right to keep and bear arms is not a right that springs forth from any power of the government under the Constitution; rather, the Second Amendment is a limitation on the government's reach into the sphere of the individual's God given right to arms. As *Heller* found, the "threat that the new Federal Government would destroy the citizens' militia by taking away their arms was the reason [the ancient right of bearing arms for self defense and hunting]—unlike some other English rights—was codified in a written Constitution."[224] In no way was the Second Amendment seen as being the source of the right to keep and bear arms; it was simply a bulwark to keep the government from infringing on that inherent right.

So the San Francisco Court (and the Sunnyvale Court as well) failed to take into account a right protected

---

[223] *Id.*

[224] *Id.*

by the Second Amendment above and beyond the right to self defense: the right to keep and bear arms for hunting.

To begin with anecdotal evidence, the author of this paper is a life-long hunter who was born in San Francisco and raised in the San Francisco Bay Area. Prior to the enactment of the draconian firearms regulations that have made California one of the most firearms-hostile state in the union[225] the author owned and used a variety of hunting arms, including those with what are now referred to as "large capacity magazines", in pursuit of all types of game. While deer hunting, the author currently carries as a protective sidearm a 9mm pistol with what is now referred to as a "large capacity magazine".[226]

---

[225] *See* the LC Report, supra note 151 ("In the last two decades, with the Law Center's dedicated team of attorneys leading the way, California has become a national leader in the movement for...gun laws.")

[226] The 9mm pistol referred to was purchased with a 12 round magazine, which was the standard factory-supplied magazine at the

It is not uncommon in California for illegal drug production facilities to be located in the rural areas that are also the state's most frequently used deer hunting zones. A recent story described the following from the deer hunting forests of Mendocino County, where the author hunts ever year:

> *The potential for so much profit has made the backcountry contested territory, with growers menacing deer hunters and firing warning shots at ranchers. In 2006, Robert Corey Want and Ivan Tillotson, Jr., two members of a local Native American tribe, were shot to death by Mexican growers cultivating a pot farm on the tribe's reservation. Two years later, in Lake County (which*

---

time of purchase in 1986. As the author does not live in either San Francisco or Sunnyvale, the continued possession of a grandfathered "large capacity magazine" remains legal, as of the date of this paper.

covers part of the Mendocino forest), a county supervisor named Rob Brown discovered two acres of hidden gardens—including one that had been booby-trapped with sharp punji sticks—scattered about his 300-acre property.

Many fearful locals have simply abandoned long-cherished trails and camping spots, and deadly firefights between growers and Mendocino cops have increased. In July 2010, a sheriff's deputy shot and killed a 24-year-old grower named Angel Hernandez-Farias during a raid in the woods. Three weeks later, Mendocino deputies raided another remote garden and killed a grower wielding a rifle. Two more growers were killed during raids in nearby counties that summer, an unprecedented level of violence in what had once been a peaceable enclave of hippies, pear farmers, and mountain recluses.

In August 2010, long-latent civic fury spilled into the open at a county board of supervisors meeting that took place in Covelo, a tiny hardscrabble town bordering the Mendocino forest and itself notorious for producing prodigious amounts of pot. A fish-and-game commissioner named Paul Trouette, who'd just spent three days in the woods, reported seeing "carloads of Hispanic cartel-type vehicles flooding the roadways." A store owner claimed the forest was under "armed foreign invasion." Two ranchers and a teacher said growers had shot at them. Shaking with rage, another rancher demanded that supervisors declare a state of emergency and use the National Guard to clear the forest, a move without precedent in U.S. history.

"It's an occupation," said the rancher, Chris Brennan. "I've been shot at. They're wiping out our deer. They're poisoning the bears. We might as well change the name to Cartel National Forest."[227]

As a byproduct of the drug cartels using hunting grounds for drug production, it is now common for hunters to come across feral pit bulls and Rottweiler dogs that had been used to protect the drug compounds but have either escaped or been released.[228]

---

[227] *See, e.g.,* Damon Tabor, *Weed Whackers*, OUTSIDE MAGAZINE (June 2012), available at http://www.outsideonline.com/outdoor-adventure/politics/Weed-Whackers-.html

[228] *See, e.g.,* Glenda Anderson, *Pit Bulls Attacking Mendocino Livestock*, THE PRESS DEMOCRAT, (Nov. 30, 2008), available at http://www.pressdemocrat.com/article/20081130/news/811300364#page=0 ("Law enforcement and agriculture officials suspect the spike in pit bull attacks on livestock and wildlife is a byproduct of the growth in marijuana production in the county. Marijuana growers are suspected of bringing many pit bulls to the area to guard the large number of pot gardens in the northern part of the county; pit bulls are

When confronted with a pack of wild dogs or drug cartel members protecting a marijuana field or methamphetamine lab, a hunter would have little chance of survival if all he or she had for self defense was a typical hunting rifle with a magazine capacity of four rounds of ammunition.[229] Anecdotally, in 2011 while field dressing game, the author was approached by a pack of coyotes who were attracted by the smell of the animal being butchered in

---

commonly found along with marijuana gardens at rural residences in the area, officials said.")

[229] The Remington 700 rifle is "...the world's most prolific bolt-action centerfire rifle of all time" with over 5,000,000 rifles produced over 50 years. Kyle Wintersteen, *The Remington 700: A Look at the Rifles Behind the 700's 50th Anniversary*, OUTDOOR LIFE (May 2012), available at http://www.outdoorlife.com/photos/gallery/guns/rifles/2012/05/remington-700-look-best-rifles-behind-700s-50th-anniversary. Though the standard magazine capacity of Remington 700 rifles varies by caliber and model, a four round magazine is typical for popular deer hunting calibers. *See* http://www.remington.com/product-families/firearms/centerfire-families/bolt-action-model-700.aspx.

the field. It took in excess of 10 rounds fired to drive all of the predators away. It is not uncommon for hunters to be confronted in the field by predators.[230] The luxury of

---

[230] *See, e.g.*, Tristan Scott, *Hunters Kill Wolf, Flee after Attack*, THE MONTANA STANDARD (Nov. 5, 2010), available at http://mtstandard.com/news/local/hunters-kill-wolf-flee-after-attack/article_3c176ed4-e89a-11df-9f32-001cc4c03286.html ("Two Flathead Valley hunters say a pack of wolves surrounded them in the woods Saturday while they attempted to retrieve a quartered bull elk, forcing them to shoot and kill a wolf before fleeing"); Jeff Humphrey, *Hunter Becomes the Hunted in Idaho Wolf Attack*, KXLY.COM (Oct. 12, 2011), available at http://www.kxly.com/news/Hunter-Becomes-The-Hunted-In-Idaho-Wolf-Attack/9226008 ("A North Idaho grandmother considers herself lucky to be alive after she was able to shoot and kill a wolf as it tried to attack her on a recent hunting trip."); James Halpin, *Rabid Wolf Attacks Hunterin Southwest Alaska*, ANCHORAGE DAILY NEWS (Sept. 18, 2009), available at http://www.adn.com/2009/09/18/940618/rabid-wolf-attacks-hunter-in-southwest.html ("Roderick Phillip and three hunting partners were at a bonfire. After about a week out along the Kuskokwim River near Kalskag, they'd already bagged a bull moose...[a wolf] lunged at his face, then bit him on the leg, and the two ended up on the ground wrestling before his brother killed it"); Sam Schultz, *Hunter Attacked by Coyote he Fooled With his Turkey Call*, NBCBAYAREA.COM (May 13, 2012), available at http://www.nbcbayarea.com/news/weird/NATL-

carrying multiple magazines and having the time to change them is not something that is often afforded in the wild when predators attack. This is especially true if the predator is a bear or mountain lion, which likely requires multiple hits in a vital region to stop (something that would require a multiple of shots to achieve, given the dexterity

---

Coyote-Turkey-Call-Hunter-Bill-Robinson-Maine-Attack-Bite-149979515.html ("[a hunter] lured a turkey-hungry coyote that lunged at and bit him, mistaking him for a turkey."); *Elk Hunter Fends Off Cougar Attack*, WASHINGTON DEP'T OF FISH AND WILDLIFE PRESS RELEASE (Nov. 3, 2003), available at http://wdfw.wa.gov/news/nov0303a/ ("An elk hunter in the Blue Mountains of southeast Washington fended off an attack by a cougar while starting to field dress a dead elk this week."); Carly Flandro, *Bear Injured Two Hunters in Madison County Wilderness Area*, BOZEMAN DAILY CHRONICLE (Nov. 14, 2011), available at http://www.bozemandailychronicle.com/news/region/article_f1da3532-0eee-11e1-b393-001cc4c03286.html ("A bear attacked and injured two men Saturday while they were hunting elk in the Lee Metcalf Wilderness.) In California alone, the California Dep't of Fish and Wildlife has documented 14 mountain lion attacks on humans between 1986 and 2013. *See Verified Mountain Lion Attacks on Humans in California (1986 through 2013)*, available at https://www.dfg.ca.gov/wildlife/lion/attacks.html.

and speed of the animal and the stress the hunter would be under).[231]

"Large capacity magazines" are also essential for the control of varmints, from prairie dogs to wild hogs. In a recent segment on the CNN show "AC360, Anderson Cooper featured a business owner who uses rifles with 30

---

[231] *See, e.g.,* Kurt Repanshek, Grizzly *Bear Shot and Killed By Hikers In Denali National Park and Preserve*, NATIONAL PARKS TRAVELER, (May 30, 2010), available at http://www.nationalparkstraveler.com/2010/05/grizzly-bear-shot-and-killed-hikers-denali-national-park-and-preserve5943. In this case, a .45 caliber semi-automatic pistol was used and all nine rounds in the magazine and chamber were fired at the bear (a .45 caliber pistol generally has a magazine capacity of eight and can be carried with an additional round in the chamber). The bear ultimately died from its wounds, but only after it turned and walked away from the hikers after being shot at. It was neither stopped nor incapacitated by the nine rounds fired at it, showing that the limited capacity in the magazine of the pistol was not sufficient to ensure the safety of the hikers. Had there been two bears present, it is clear that the hikers would not have been able to defend themselves with the limited capacity magazine in the pistol.

round magazines to control hog populations.[232] When it comes to prairie dog control, the preeminent sportsman's magazine Outdoor Life recently listed the DPMS Panther Bull 24 Special, a rifle that comes from the factory with a 30 round magazine, as its top pick.[233]

---

[232] AC360, *AR-15s used to Protect Crops from Hogs* (Mar. 22, 2013), available at http://ac360.blogs.cnn.com/2013/03/22/ar-15s-used-to-protect-crops-from-hogs/. After explaining that hogs cause $1.5 billion in crop damage per year in the United States, the show's correspondent stated that a 30 round magazine would be needed to adequately deal with a sow with young pigs. See transcript at http://newsbusters.org/blogs/pj-gladnick/2013/03/28/cnn-correspondent-touts-ar-15s-wild-hog-hunting-then-wonders-why-hunter.

[233] Bryce Towley, *Best Rifles for Hunting Prairie Dogs*, OUTDOOR LIFE (June 2011), available at http://www.outdoorlife.com/photos/gallery/hunting/2011/06/best-rifles-hunting-prairie-dogs?photo=1#node-1001346386. Details on the DPMS Panther Bull 24 Special are available at various firearms retailer s' website. The following description is from http://www.cheaperthandirt.com/product/61636: "The DPMS Panther Bull 24 Special has a 416 stainless steel 24" fluted bull barrel, 6 grooves, right hand 1:9" twist, button rifled, gas operated rotating bolt, and a 8620 steel bolt carrier. The A3 flat top upper receiver

Quantifying the lawful use of "large capacity magazines" is, unfortunately, as difficult as quantifying the lawful incidences of speech. It is only when a right is abused or used in an unlawful way that there is any semblance of recordkeeping. However, as the Sunnyvale Order documented, "…47 percent of all magazines owned are capable of holding more than ten rounds…."[234] Of these millions of "large capacity magazines" in use, the Sunnyvale Court was only able to identify a handful of criminal misuses of the magazines. Thus, it has to be the case that compared to the annual average of 18 mass

---

features a dust cover and a shell deflector. The upper and lower receiver made of 7075-T6 aircraft aluminum. The lower receiver features a semi-auto trigger group, aluminum trigger guard, and aluminum magazine release button. The stock is a standard A2 black Zytel, with trap door assembly. The handguard is aluminum ribbed with free float tube and the pistol grip is a Panther Tactical grip. **Each rifle comes with two (2) 30 round magazines,** nylon web sling. " (emphasis added)

[234] Sunnyvale Order, supra note 2, at 10.

shooting deaths or even the estimated 228 "large capacity magazine" related homicides in California, there are millions of incidences of lawful "large capacity magazine" uses each year.

Consequently, it is nearly impossible to empirically determine what percent of uses of "large capacity magazines" are in furtherance of violent crime generally or mass shootings in particular, but it's clear that the incidence of criminal use is infinitesimal, well under 1%.[235]

---

[235] According to the expert study cited in the Sunnyvale Order, guns equipped "large capacity magazines" were used in approximately 18% of crimes and made up about 18% of the civilian handgun population (it is important to note that only pistols have magazines; revolvers use cylinders to hold ammunition). Christopher S. Koper, *An Updated Assessment of the Federal Assault Weapons Ban: Impacts on Gun Markets and Gun Violence, 1994-2003* (June 2004) at 18, available at https://www.ncjrs.gov/pdffiles1/nij/grants/204431.pdf From this it follows that, "large capacity magazines" are not over-represented in criminal activity involving handguns generally. We would have to find out what percent of all guns that are lawfully owned are used in criminal activity in order to find out what 18% of that number

This is a critical point for both District Court Orders, as they compared the percent of "large capacity magazines" used in mass shootings or homicides in general to an inapposite bit of data: the average number of rounds fired in self defense. In order to determine whether "large capacity magazines" posed an unreasonable risk to society, the proper comparison would have been to compare the

---

represents, and such data are not available. The best approximation available is that there are approximately 114 million privately owned handguns in the United States and approximately 6,000 homicides each year attributable to handguns. Alpers, Philip, Amélie Rossetti, Daniel Salinas, Marcus Wilson. 2014. *Guns in the United States: Firearms, armed violence and gun law*. SYDNEY SCHOOL OF PUBLIC HEALTH, THE UNIVERSITY OF SYDNEY. GunPolicy.org,. accessed 5 April 2014. at: http://www.gunpolicy.org/firearms/region/united-states. Using this data, the percent of all handguns legally owned in the United States that are used in homicides is .005%, which would mean that the percentage of "large capacity magazine" equipped handguns legally owned in the United States that are used in homicides is .0009%. Of course, this only accounts for homicides and not all shootings, but since the Magazine Bans were predicated on the desire to prevent deaths, the .0009% figure is a reasonable datapoint to use.

frequency with which "large capacity magazines" are used or possessed in mass shootings to the frequency with which they are used or possessed for lawful purposes, including hunting. In other words, the District Courts would have had to examine the percentage of self defense incidents where a "large capacity magazine" was involved, without regard to the number of shots that were fired from it, in order to have an appropriate comparison to the number of times a "large capacity magazine" was involved in a mass shooting.

The obvious reason this wasn't done is that there are no data on the number of times a "large capacity magazine" has been used in a self defense incident and the best estimates are that less than 1% of all "large capacity magazines" are involved in any violent criminal activity, let alone murders, let alone mass shootings. So in an attempt to prevent something that happens with minimal frequency, the District Court Orders were willing to prevent the masses from exercising an enumerated constitutional right.

What is the precedent for this? It certainly can't be found in civic responses to AIDS or violent video games or motor vehicle casualties or even in school bus accidents, bicycle accidents, hernias or obesity, all of which have higher rates of fatalities than "large capacity magazines".

(a) The District Court Orders compared to Morales

Returning to *Morales* (where the Supreme Court struck down Chicago's gang assembly prohibition), a Centers for Disease Control study estimated that approximately 30% of homicides in large cities are gang-related.[236] In a 2011 Federal Bureau of Investigation study on the threat of gangs the following was observed:

---

[236] U.S DEP'T OF HEALTH AND HUMAN SERVICES, CENTERS FOR DISEASE CONTROL, *Gang Homicides — Five U.S. Cities, 2003–2008*, (hereinafter, the "CDC Gang Report") available at http://www.cdc.gov/mmwr/preview/mmwrhtml/mm6103a2.htm#tab1. This study examined five cities with large street gang populations and found that of the 2,933 homicides in the study period, 856 were gang related. This estimate is on the low end of studies attempting to determine the role gang homicides play in the overall homicide rate. Other studies have indicated that the rate may be as high as 80%. *See*, Jason Howerton, *The Blaze Fact-Checks ABC: Did Diane Sawyer Use Misleading Stats in '20/20' Report on Children and Guns?*, published at BLAZE.COM on Jan. 31, 2014, available at http://www.theblaze.com/stories/2014/01/31/theblaze-fact-checks-abc-did-diane-sawyer-use-misleading-stats-in-2020-report-on-children-and-guns/ (fact-checking an ABC news feature and asserting that up to 80% of homicides are gang related). *See, also*, Evan DeFilippis, *Do We Have a Gang Problem or a Gun Problem?*, published at the HUFFINGTON POST BLOG on April 3, 2014, available at http://www.huffingtonpost.com/evan-defilippis/do-we-have-a-gang-problem_b_5071639.html (disputing the Blaze.com assertion that 80% of homicides are gang related but accepting the CDC Gang Report figure of approximately 30%).

[g]angs are becoming increasingly savvy and are embracing new and advanced technology to facilitate criminal activity and enhance their criminal operations. Prepaid cell phones, social networking and microblogging websites, VoIP systems, virtual worlds, and gaming systems enable gang members to communicate globally and discreetly. **Gangs are also increasingly employing advanced countermeasures to monitor and target law enforcement while engaging in a host of criminal activity.**

…

Gang members routinely utilize the Internet to communicate with one another, recruit, promote their gang, intimidate rivals and police, conduct gang business, showcase illegal exploits, and facilitate criminal activity such as drug trafficking, extortion, identity theft, money laundering, and prostitution. Social networking, microblogging, and video-sharing websites—such as Facebook, YouTube, and Twitter—are now more accessible, versatile, and allow tens of thousands of gang members to easily communicate, recruit, and form new gang alliances nationwide and worldwide.

NGIC reporting indicates that a majority of gang members use the Internet for recruitment, gang promotion, and cyber-bullying or intimidation. Many also use the Internet for identity theft, computer hacking, and phishing schemes.

…

The proliferation of social networking websites has made gang activity more prevalent and lethal—moving gangs from the streets into cyber space. Gang members, criminals, and drug traffickers are using the Internet not only to recruit and build their social networks, but to expand and operate their criminal networks without the proximity once needed for communication

...

According to information obtained from multiple state and federal law enforcement sources, incarcerated gang members are accessing micro-blogging and social networking web sites such as MocoSpace and Twitter with smuggled prepaid cellular telephones and using the messaging features to coordinate criminal activity.[237]

Following the logic of the District Court Orders, any city with gang violence would be free to ban cell

---

[237] FEDERAL BUREAU OF INVESTIGATION, U.S. NATIONAL GANG INTELLIGENCE CENTER, *2011 National Gang Threat Assessment – Emerging Trends* at page 41-42, available at http://www.fbi.gov/stats-services/publications/2011-national-gang-threat-assessment/2011-national-gang-threat-assessment-emerging-trends (emphasis added).

phones, computers and social networking (as well as colored clothing, the use of hand signs and perhaps even rap music). Such a ban would be a total ban, not just a ban directed at proven gang members. If this sounds hard to believe, one simply needs to go back to the District Court Orders to see that they were blanket prohibitions on the ownership of "large capacity magazines". It didn't matter whether a person had a criminal record or some other indicia of likely misuse of the magazine. The ban applies to everyone.

A city implementing such a ban could point out, as the District Courts did, that banning cell phones, computers and social networking was not a ban on speech; it is simply a ban on certain subsets of speech, leaving many other avenues, such as NSA-monitored landlines or conversations while on line at supermarkets, open for those who wished to engage in lawful communication.

Yet, in looking at *Morales*, it is clear that a ban of this nature would be struck down immediately. Whether such a ban were to fall on First Amendment grounds or, as in *Morales*, for being constitutionally vague, the effect and basis would be the same. The Supreme Court is understandably reticent to second guess legislative acts when it can predicate a ruling on other grounds, which is what it did in *Morales*, but the Court made it clear that the enforcement of existing laws directed at underlying criminal conduct was the proper way for Chicago to handle gang violence.[238] Justice Stevens explicitly stated as much: "if the loitering is in fact harmless and innocent, the

---

[238] *See Morales, supra* note 91 at 52 and note 17, where the Court explained that there was no need for the law in question because it was simply duplicative and over inclusive of otherwise lawful activity (citing to testimony at a community hearing on the law where a representative of the police acknowledged that then-existing laws gave the police authority to arrest 90% of the people engaging in the targeted conduct).

dispersal order itself is an unjustified impairment of liberty."[239] Likewise, prohibiting the mere possession of a "large capacity magazine" that is being used for otherwise lawful purposes would be an unjustified impairment of liberty (and of an enumerated constitutional right).

There is no question that the provisions of the California Penal Code that prohibit, *inter alia*, assault, homicide, the use of a firearm in the commission of a felony and the discharge of a firearm within city limits[240] apply to San Francisco and Sunnyvale, so both cities have ample authority, without the Magazine Bans, to prosecute

---

[239] *Id.* at 58.

[240] *See, e.g.*, CALIFORNIA PENAL CODE §§ 187-199 (prohibiting murder); CALIFORNIA PENAL CODE §§ 12001-12022.95 (prohibiting the possession of a firearm while engaging in felonies); SAN FRANCISCO PARK CODE § 4.01(b) (prohibiting the carrying or firing of firearms). In fact, CALIFORNIA PENAL CODE §29800-29830 provides for an outright ban on the ownership or possession of firearms by persons convicted of felonies and certain misdemeanors.

those who engage in the targeted conduct.

Thus, applying *Morales* to the Magazine Bans should result in a ruling that the laws are either overbroad, in that they are over-inclusive of otherwise lawful uses of "large capacity magazines," or that they are blatant infringements of the Second Amendment.

As we'll see with the analysis of *Brown*, when government is attempting to predict unlawful behavior and implement prophylactic restrictions to prevent such behavior, the empirical threshold is even higher.

(b) The District Court Orders compared to *Brown*

It is in the final line of the quoted texted from *Turner* in the *Brown* opinion *("when trenching on first amendment interests, even incidentally, the government must be able to adduce either empirical support or at least sound reasoning on behalf of its measures")*[241] that San Francisco and Sunnyvale should fail in defending the Magazine Bans.

As the Supreme Court suggested in its *Heller* opinion,[242] First Amendment principles should form the basis for Second Amendment inquiries. Even with an intermediate scrutiny review, which is likely too lax for

---

[241] *See* text accompanying *supra* note 110

[242] *Heller*, slip op. at 22 ("Of course the right was not unlimited, just as the First Amendment's
right of free speech was not…. Thus, we do not read the Second Amendment to protect the right of citizens to carry arms for any sort of confrontation, just as we do not read the First Amendment to protect the right of citizens to speak for any purpose."). For an in-depth discussion of a proposal to apply First Amendment constitutional review principles to Second Amendment cases *see* Eugene Volokh, *Implementing the Right To Keep and Bear Arms for Self Defense: An Analytical Framework and a Research Agenda*, 56 UCLA L. Rev. 1443 (2009).

what is, as the Sunnyvale Court acknowledged, an absolute ban on a type of arm subject to the protections of the Second Amendment, the Magazine Bans are unsupportable. The legislative findings used as justification for the Magazine Bans were based on extreme suppositions of a worst case scenario, ignoring volumes of relevant data that would undermine the public safety claims of the respective cities, while relying upon flawed and incomplete data that served to rubber stamp the foregone conclusions of the sponsors of the Magazine Bans. This is clearly anathema to *Turner*, a case decided using intermediate scrutiny, and *Brown*, a case decided using strict scrutiny.

As California did in *Brown*, both San Francisco and Sunnyvale ignored far more immediate and serious threats to public safety to focus on one item that had virtually no impact on overall levels of public safety, inspired, apparently, by a populist meme. Indeed, while the District

Court Orders made note of the fact that there were alternatives available for self defense even if "large capacity magazines" were prohibited, a claim that there are other forms of video games available other than violent ones would not have altered the decision of the *Brown* court.

And more troubling as a matter of constitutional law, the District Court Orders represent an unprecedented reversal of the burden of proof. While relying on what can at best be characterized as irrelevant data of dubious reliability presented by the respective cities, the District Courts required the citizens to prove that they had a need for the arms that even the Sunnyvale Court acknowledged were subject to the protections of the Second Amendment. Though the Sunnyvale Court accepted the city's evidence without question or inquiry, it dismissed the evidence presented by the plaintiffs, calling it "anecdotal."[243]

As an initial matter, the traditional methods of judicial review for constitutional questions, rational basis, intermediate scrutiny and strict scrutiny, all represent a longstanding concept of burdens of proof. At the intermediate scrutiny and strict scrutiny levels of judicial review it has been clearly established that the burden of proof is on the government[244] and then, only after the government's burden has been met is the affected individual or entity required to rebut the government's position.

---

[243] Sunnyvale Order, *supra* note 2, at 14-15.

[244] *See* Russell W. Galloway, *Means-End Scrutiny in American Constitutional Law*, 21 LOY. L.A. L. REV. 449, 452-458 (1988). While it is clear that the government will have the burden of proof in intermediate scrutiny and strict scrutiny cases, Galloway argues that there are some rational basis cases that may also place the burden of proof on the government. Id. at 452.

In the District Court Orders, the burden should have been on the government to prove that the "large capacity magazines" presented an unreasonable risk to the public. While the District Courts nominally established this threshold burden, the government presented no such evidence and, in fact, each city's evidence showed how rare mass shootings and criminal incidents involving "large capacity magazines" are. The other evidence presented by each city was nonsensical and presented purely for shock value, as it only showed that "large capacity magazines" were used in some notorious crimes, but it failed to qualify that point with the overarching evidence that the criminal misuse of "large capacity magazines" was approaching or under 1% of all lawful uses thereof.[245]

In *Brown*, the State of California failed to meet its burden of proof, notwithstanding its presentation of

---

[245] *See* text accompanying *supra* note 43.

numerous shocking examples of violent behavior correlated to violent video games. In the Magazine Cases, neither San Francisco nor Sunnyvale could do any better than present some shocking and very isolated incidents of "large capacity magazine" misuse, but those examples were not even correlational, let alone proof of causation.

Since neither city was able to demonstrate that "large capacity magazines" posed an unreasonable risk to public safety, the District Courts should have stopped the inquiry at that point and rule against each respective city for failing to have met their respective burdens of proof. Instead, the District Courts devoted copious attention to the alleged failure of the challengers to prove that there was a need for "large capacity magazines".

Imagine what, for example, First Amendment cases would look like if the burden were on the challenger of a law to prove there was a need for speech or assembly or the exercise of religion. Or even more troubling, imagine if a woman who chose to terminate a pregnancy were required to present proof of her need to abort the child.

(c) The District Court Orders compared to the SDNY Opinion

If the standards used in the District Court Orders were to have been used in SDNY Opinion, New York City would still have its Stop and Frisk Policy in effect. The SDNY Opinion, as a reminder, found that the fact that 6% of cases where the policy was implemented resulted in an infringement of individuals' Fourth Amendment rights was enough to strike down the policy. With the Magazine Bans 100% of the citizens who desire to retain possession of their otherwise lawful "large capacity magazines" will have their Second Amendment Rights infringed, without either city being required to show that the magazines were being used to commit crimes.

(d) The District Court Orders Compared to *Perry*

In *Perry*, the 9th Circuit invalidated an amendment to the California Constitution that had been approved by a majority of California's voters in an election with a historically high voter turnout. The *Perry* court, even using the lax standard of rational review, found that a right that was neither enumerated in the Constitution nor even recognized by the Supreme Court could not be infringed by voters who, in more than one instance, had explicitly voted to not recognize the right. The *Perry* court defended the rights of a minority against what it saw to be the baseless fears of the majority.

While the San Francisco Magazine Ban was enacted

without voter approval, the Sunnyvale Magazine Ban received the support of a few thousand voters in an election with very light voter turnout and this support was noted by the Sunnyvale Court as a reason to deny the injunction. This, clearly, is contrary to *Perry*, which found no dispositive effect to voter support for a challenged law (or constitutional amendment, in the case of *Perry*).

Under *Perry*, then, it would be hard to imagine the court upholding either Magazine Ban, especially since the bans represent an infringement of an enumerated, constitutional right and the evidence used to portray "large capacity magazines" as a public health menace was demonstrably based on baseless, politically motivated fear mongering rather than factual analysis.

Moreover, *Perry* stands for the proposition that courts should disregard the will and acts of voters and elected representatives in favor of protecting vilified minority rights, even rights that the court hasn't even recognized.

(e) The District Court Orders compared to *Hill* and *Schenck*

In neither *Hill* nor *Schenck* were absolute prohibitions upheld. *Hill* did allow for a limited infringement on First Amendment speech rights, but that infringement didn't prevent protesters from uttering the words of their choice or voicing those words in the direct vicinity of their intended audience. In fact, the *Hill* court took pains to point out that in no way would the protesters be thwarted in their attempts to communicate with abortion clinic visitors. *Schenck* struck down a speech restriction that had the effect of substantively impairing a protester's right to communicate with his or her intended audience. The Magazine Bans, of course, effect an absolute infringement on the Second Amendment right and no provision is made to ensure that individuals are afforded substantially similar alternatives.

If a court were to employ the standards used in the District Court Orders with regard to abortion clinic protests there would be absolute bans on all protests anywhere near abortion clinics. Potential protesters would be told that their speech is nothing more than a subset of the right to speak and the speakers could still communicate their messages anywhere other than near an abortion clinic. This is at odds with *Schenck* but it is precisely the logic used by the District Courts.

(f) The District Court Orders Compared to Government Responses to the AIDS Epidemic

The most striking, and likely most controversial, comparison to the District Court Orders is the government response to the AIDS epidemic. By any count, AIDS has been a devastating killer. Over the past 30 years, over 35 million people have been killed by AIDS worldwide.[246] Though the spread of the epidemic has been slowed, AIDS still took 1.6 million lives worldwide in 2012.[247] In the United States for the same 30 year period, approximately 636,000 people have been killed by AIDS, with over 19,000 deaths alone in 2010.[248] Over 95,000 of the total United States AIDS fatalities have been in California,[249] with over 19,000 of those being in San Francisco.[250]

The following is a chart comparing AIDS fatalities over the past 30 years[251] to various types of firearms-

---

[246] *Global AIDS Overview* page of AIDS Informational Website, *supra* note 114

[247] *Id.*

[248] KFF 2010 Report, *supra* note 158.

[249] 2013 CA AIDS Report, *supra* note 163.

[250] SF AIDS Website, *supra* note 164.

[251] For the period ending 2010, except as otherwise indicated.

related fatalities for the same period.

	AIDS Fatalities	Mass Shootings	Firearms Homicides	"Large Capacity Magazine" Fatalities
United States	636,000	547	476,00[252]	80,932[253]
California	95,000	66[254]	57,540[255]	9,782[256]

---

[252] Estimated. This figure was arrived at by assuming that the annual firearms homicide rate for the first 20 years of the period was 18,253 and for the final 10 years was 11,101, based on a report titled *Firearms Violence, 1993-2011* issued by the U.S. DEP'T. OF JUSTICE, BUREAU OF JUSTICE STATISTICS, issued on May 7, 2013 and available at http://www.bjs.gov/content/pub/press/fv9311pr.cfm.

[253] Based on an estimate of 17% of all firearms homicides being related to "large capacity magazines". *See supra* note 154.

[254] Estimated based on the proportion of approximately 12% reflected in the estimated number of firearms homicides in the United States as compared to California in this table. As California represents 12% of the population of the entire United States (see http://quickfacts.census.gov/qfd/states/06000.html) this number is a conservative, yet reasonable, estimate. A CNN report listing the 25 most deadly mass shootings in the United States since 1965 (available at http://www.cnn.com/2013/09/16/us/20-deadliest-mass-shootings-in-u-s-history-fast-facts/) listed a total of 37 mass shooting fatalities in California for that period. This report only included mass shootings with at least 8 fatalities, while the CRS Report defines a Mass Shooting

While AIDS is an indiscriminate killer, it strikes one group of people particularly hard. The latest data show that "…[a]lthough [gay, bisexual, and other men who have sex with men (MSM)] represent about 4% of the male population in the United States, in 2010, MSM accounted for 78% of new HIV infections among males and 63% of all new infections. MSM accounted for 52% of all people living with HIV infection in 2009, the most recent year these data are available."[257]

Using the 63% rate as a baseline we can estimate

---

as one resulting in at least 4 fatalities, not including the perpetrator. Thus, the 66 fatality estimate is conservative, if not excessive.

[255] Estimated. This figure was arrived at by using the 1,342 figure from the study cited at note 153 herein for the final 10 years and 2,206 (1,342 increased by 60%, which is what 18,253 is compared to 11,101).

[256] Based on an estimate of 17% of all firearms homicides being related to "large capacity magazines". *See supra* note 154

[257] *U.S. Statistics* page of AIDS Informational Website, *supra* note 114

the number of AIDS deaths that have been related to homosexual sexual activity.[258] The number of fatalities in the United States and California, specifically, on an annual and cumulative basis are estimated as follows.

	California	United States
Annual[259]	1,025[260]	12,182[261]
30 Year Total[262]	59,850	400,680

Based on this estimated data, 12,182 deaths in the United States and 1,025 deaths in California each year can be attributed to the activity of a group that makes up less

---

[258] For California, the 63% rate likely undercounts the number of AIDS deaths attributable to homosexual sexual activity, since a recent report found that "75.7% of all HIV/AIDS cases occur among gay men" in California. SF AIDS Website, *supra* note 164.

[259] Estimated, based on the 2010 data, KFF 2010 Report, *supra* note 158.

[260] Based on an estimate of 63% of the 1,627 deaths reported in the 2010 KFF Report, *supra* note 158

[261] Based on an estimate of 63% of the 19,338 deaths reported in the 2010 KFF Report, *supra* note 158.

[262] Based on an estimate of the California and United States data contained in the immediately preceding chart herein.

than 2% of the population.[263]

Comparing the number of fatalities in California estimated to be attributable to homosexual sexual activity with the number of fatalities in the state estimated to be attributable to either "large capacity magazines" or mass shootings, or even all firearms-related homicides, reveals an interesting comparative statistic.

---

[263] According to the United States Census Bureau, men made of 49.2 of the nation's population in 2010. Lindsay M. Howden and Julie A. Mayer, *Age and Sex Composition: 2010*, C2010BR-03, published May 2011 by the UNITED STATES CENSUS BUREAU, available at http://www.census.gov/prod/cen2010/briefs/c2010br-03.pdf. 49.2% of the 4% of men engaging in MSM, as cited in the text accompanying *supra* note 250 equals 1.9% of the population. The percent of California's population that is homosexual is approximately the same as the nation's overall percentage (Gary J. Gates, *How many people are lesbian, gay, bisexual, and transgender?* (April 2011), THE WILLIAMS INSTITUTE ON SEXUAL ORIENTATION AND GENDER IDENTITY LAW AND PUBLIC POLICY AT UCLA SCHOOL OF LAW available at http://williamsinstitute.law.ucla.edu/wp-content/uploads/Gates-How-Many-People-LGBT-Apr-2011.pdf) (estimating the percentage of California's population that is lesbian, gay or bisexual at 3.2%. *Id.* at 5.)

	Homosexual Sexual Activity Fatalities	"Large Capacity Magazines" Fatalities	Mass Shootings	All Firearms Related Homicides
Annual	1,025	228	2[264]	1,342
Cumulative	59,850	9,782[265]	66	57,540

If public safety, and preventing fatalities in particular, were the actual objective of the cities of San Francisco and Sunnyvale, or California in general, it is clear that they have made a monumental error in targeting the more significant risk to public safety.

While this section has focused on comparing the risk of AIDS to the risk of firearms, similar comparisons, with similar results, could be made between motor vehicles

---

[264] Assuming that of the estimated 66 mass shooting fatalities for California in the past 30 years the annual rate is proportional each year.

[265] *See supra* notes 253 and 254 for an explanation of why the number is in excess of 30 multiplied by the 228 annual figure.

and firearms and obesity and firearms, among others.[266] The focus in this section on AIDS, however, is to illustrate how an activity engaged in by a small segment of the population, and one that could be subject to strict bans and stifling regulations, such as exist currently for firearms, is responsible for far more fatalities, at far higher costs to society[267], than firearms.

---

[266] *See* text and table accompany *supra* notes 156 and 167.

[267] Hutchinson, Angela B PhD, MPH; Farnham, Paul G PhD; Dean, Hazel D ScD, MPH; Ekwueme, Donatus U PhD; del Rio, Carlos MD; Kamimoto, Laurie MD, MPH; Kellerman, Scott E MD, MPH, *The Economic Burden of HIV in the United States in the Era of Highly Active Antiretroviral Therapy: Evidence of Continuing Racial and Ethnic Differences*, 43 JOURNAL OF ACQUIRED IMMUNE DEFICIENCY SYNDROMES 451 (2006) (finding the "…cost of new HIV infections in the United States in 2002 is estimated at $36.4 billion, including $6.7 billion in direct medical costs and $29.7 billion in productivity losses.") Contrast this with "[t]he total firearm assault injury cost for US hospitals in 2010 was just under $630 million." Embry M. Howell & Peter Abraham, *The Hospital Costs of Firearms Assaults* URBAN INSTITUTE PUBLICATION (Sept. 2013) at 4, available at http://www.urban.org/UploadedPDF/412894-The-Hospital-Costs-of-Firearm-Assaults.pdf.

However, the government response to AIDS has been inapposite to the government response to mass shootings, "large capacity magazines" or even firearms related homicides generally. Homosexual sexual activity has never been banned, nor regulated (beyond the regulation of conduct in public bathhouses). The government response to AIDS was massive funding of research into the cause of the disease and the potential cures for it as well as the encouragement of education regarding controlling the spread of the disease.[268] In fiscal 2014 alone, the United States budget included nearly $30 billion dollars devoted to national and global AIDS/HIV initiatives, the bulk of that amount going to care and

---

[268] THE HENRY J. KAISER FAMILY FOUNDATION FACT SHEET, U.S. FEDERAL FUNDING FOR HIV/AIDS: THE PRESIDENT'S FY 2014 BUDGET REQUEST (January 2014) (the "KFF 2014 Funding Report"), available at http://kaiserfamilyfoundation.files.wordpress.com/2014/01/7029-09-u-s-federal-funding-for-hivaids-the-presidents-fy-2014-budget-request.pdf.

treatment of AIDS patients.[269] Yet despite the cost in lives and money, the most extreme action taken by any branch of the California government to prevent the activity that was a major contributor to the spread of the disease, the temporary closure of gay bathhouses in San Francisco, lasted for a short period of time and was never repeated. Indeed, the government response to AIDS has been focused on treating the disease rather than preventing it.[270] Certainly, the government could have imposed an outright ban on homosexual sexual activity, using the same logic as the Sunnyvale Order that it only affected a subset of all sexual activity available to homosexuals and homosexuals could still engage in heterosexual sex.[271]

---

[269] *Id.* at 2.

[270] *Id.* at 3, highlighting the fact that spending on domestic AIDS prevention is "the smallest category" of the federal AIDS funding budget.

[271] This is obviously an extreme example of the Sunnyvale Court's logic, but it is only extreme because of the logic employed by the Sunnyvale Court in arguing why a ban on what it acknowledged to be a

Alternatively, the government could have identified and targeted the private analog to the gay bathhouses: online sex solicitation forums. Perhaps the most well known online sex solicitation forum is the Craigslist website. According to a recent study, the Craigslist website is responsible for a 15.9% increase in HIV cases and over

---

protected type of arm could be constitutionally permissible. The Sunnyvale Court went so far as acknowledging that 47 percent of all magazines that were privately owned were "large capacity magazine" but allowed the ban on such magazines since they represented less than a majority of all magazines. A similar case could be made that homosexual sexual activity represents a far lower proportion of all sexual activity occurring in the United States. The inanity of such a position is best illustrated by Jen Kirkman, who wrote "What if I were gay and someone said to me 'You'll change your mind"? Would you agree and suggest that I should say "You're right; I will probably stop being gay once I get this immature loving-the-same-sex thing out of my system'?" Jen Kirkman, I CAN BARELY TAKE CARE OF MYSELF: TALES FROM A HAPPY LIFE WITHOUT KIDS 197 (Simon & Schuster 2013). That is to say, the idea of fungible subsets as the basis for legal discrimination, whether it happens to be magazine size for firearms or sexual activity, is not only without precedent, it is without logic.

6,000 new HIV cases each year can be attributed to the personal ads soliciting casual sex on Craigslist.[272] If 18 annual casualties, nationwide, from mass shootings justify the infringement of the enumerated constitutional right to bear arms, the approximately 12,000 annual AIDS deaths nationally should, under the standards set by the District Court Orders, substantiate a federal shutdown of the Craigslist personals section.

This has obviously not been done, nor has it even been proposed in any form of legislation. Meanwhile, in response to the far less deadly threat posed by mass shootings and "large capacity magazines", California has imposed outright bans on entire classes of firearms and

---

[272] Jason Chan and Anindya Ghose, *Internet's Dirty Secret: Assessing the Impact of Online Intermediaries on HIV Transmission*, 38 MIS QUARTERLY (forthcoming June 2014) at 5, available at http://papers.ssrn.com/sol3/papers.cfm?abstract_id=2035585.

magazines, created such hurdles to the purchase of other firearms as to be a de facto ban on many other types of firearms and put virtually all other aspects of the purchase, sale and use of firearms and their accessories under strict government control.[273]

As an example, the following table includes a sample of state-wide regulations on firearms ownership.

---

[273] This table of laws was derived from the Wikipedia page titled "Gun Laws in California", retrieved on April 11, 2014, available at http://en.wikipedia.org/wiki/Gun_laws_in_California (on file with the author).

Subject of regulation	Provisions of regulation	Statutory reference
"Assault weapons"	Prohibition on the sale, transfer and ownership of "assault weapons" unless owned prior to effective date of law.	Penal Code §§ 30500-30530
"Large capacity magazines"	Prohibition on the sale, transfer and ownership of "large capacity magazines" unless owned prior to effective date of law.	Penal Code §§ 32310-32390
Purchase restrictions generally	Prohibits the sale of any handgun that is not approved by the state, requires the purchase of a locking device at time of purchase of firearm, requires the purchase of a state issued certificate prior to the purchase of a handgun, various fees totaling up to $100 per weapon for all firearms purchases. Waiting period of 10 days prior to taking possession of firearm. Limit of one handgun purchase in any 30 day period.	Penal Code §23635, §26500, §26850, §27540, §§31610-31670, §32000.
Firearms transportation limitations	Handguns can not be transported unless they are unloaded and in a locked container. Open carry of firearms prohibited. Concealed carry of firearms extremely limited, at discretion of law enforcement.	Penal Code §25610, §26350
Microstamping	All new semi-automatic handguns must include a device that stamps identifying information on cases of fired rounds.[274]	Penal Code §31910

---

[274] The technology, known as "microstamping", is not in common use in any other state and in combination with the requirement that new handguns for sale in California be subject to a battery of tests (CAL. PENAL CODE § 32015) that are *sui generis* to California has resulted in

Countless additional bills with provisions designed to infringe upon the right to keep and bear arms are introduced in the California legislature every year. In 2013, 17 such bills went from the legislature to the governor's desk,[275] where the governor signed 11 of them into law, including an outright ban on the most commonly used type of hunting ammunition and further bans on "large capacity

---

the imposition of such a hurdle to doing business in the State of California that many firearms manufacturers no longer sell their products in the state, resulting in a constructive ban on many types of arms. *See*, Edvard Pettersson, *California Gun Law Assailed As Back-Door Ban In Court*, BLOOMBERG.COM (Feb 7. 2014), available at http://www.bloomberg.com/news/2014-02-07/california-gun-law-assailed-as-back-door-ban-in-court.html.

[275] *See* Valerie Richardson, *California's great gun grab: State's sweeping gun control bills target firearms, ammo — and hunting; Lead bullet ban could end hunting, critics warn*, Wash. Times (Sept. 20, 2013), available at
http://www.washingtontimes.com/news/2013/sep/20/californias-great-gun-grab-states-sweeping-gun-con/#ixzz2ybmeN7UM

magazines".[276] It is no exaggeration when anti-firearms advocates call California the most aggressive state in the union when it comes to imposing restrictions on the right to keep and bear arms.[277] When taken together, California's regulatory scheme is tantamount to a constructive ban on the most popular firearms, and arms generally, in the rest of the country.

Unlike the response to AIDS, where the government never intruded upon non-public sexual conduct, the government (in California and elsewhere) has made no distinction between its regulation of firearms that are used privately and firearms used publicly. That is, while the regulations affecting bathhouses did put some restrictions

---

[276] Peter Fimrite and Will Kane, *Jerry Brown Signs 11 Gun-related Laws, Vetoes Seven*, SFGATE.com, (Oct. 12, 2013), available at http://www.sfgate.com/news/article/Jerry-Brown-signs-11-gun-related-laws-vetoes-4889448.php.

[277] LC Report, *supra* note 151.

on homosexual sexual activity, those regulations were only applicable to homosexual sexual activity in public baths. Conduct occurring in private was and is unregulated. The temporary closure of gay bathhouses, where AIDS found a breeding ground, was dismissed as "arbitrary" and without "a basis in public health."[278] At the very least, the Magazine Bans are no less arbitrary or without basis in public health.

If firearms were regulated in this manner, there would be no bans on any types of weapons and only the use of firearms in public (e.g., when carrying a handgun in public or using a firearm for hunting on public land) would be subject to any regulation. That would mean that if a person sought to have a "large capacity magazine" or "assault weapon" in his home or on other private property, such as a privately owned ranch, it would be at the person's

---

[278] *See supra* note 126 and accompanying text.

discretion, with no government intervention or restrictions.

Similarly, if motor vehicles were regulated on the same basis as firearms, SUVs would be banned because they have similar cosmetic features to military vehicles[279] and any vehicle that had the ability to travel at speeds in excess of a specified miles per hour (the exact number being determined by the speed at which a majority of accidents occur) would be confiscated en masse.

Instead, current law regulates the misuse of motor vehicles, rather than banning their possession and use

---

[279] *See* Jacob Sollum, *What's an Assault Weapon?*, REASON MAGAZINE (Jan. 30, 2013), available at http://reason.com/archives/2013/01/30/whats-an-assault-weapon (pointing out that the primary similarity between "assault weapons" available to civilians and military versions of such weapons: "The distinguishing characteristics of 'assault weapons' are mainly cosmetic and have little or no functional significance in the context of mass shootings or ordinary gun crimes.")

outright. If a person wants a car capable of achieving speeds of more than 260 miles per hour[280] or an SUV that looks like and has the same general performance of a military utility vehicle,[281] he or she can buy and use it on public roads, subject to laws relating to speed, place of use and method of use. None of these laws constitute anything remotely resembling the constructive or actual bans on arms. Moreover, the motor vehicle regulations generally apply only to the use of vehicles on public roads and do not apply to vehicles when they are used on private property. If firearms laws were of such a nature, a citizen would have

---

[280] *See* Justin Lloyd-Miller, 11 Fastest Street Legal Cars in the World, Wall St. Cheat Sheet (Jan. 8, 2014), available at http://wallstcheatsheet.com/stocks/10-fastest-road-legal-cars-in-the-world.html/?a=viewall (listing 11 cars available for purchase and use on streets in the United States, with tops speeds ranging from 220 miles per hour for the Lamborghini Aventador to 267 miles per hour for the Bugatti Veyron Super Sport.

[281] *See* the comparison of the civilian and military versions of the "Hummer" utility vehicle at http://www.amgeneral.com/vehicles/hummer/compare.php.

no restrictions on using "assault weapons" at a private firing range or on any other private property.

One new regulation that had been proposed in California is a requirement that all firearms owners maintain liability insurance, with proponents arguing that this requirement already applies to motor vehicles, so it's not unreasonable to have a similar requirement for firearms.[282] Like many other proposed and enacted firearms regulations, the fact that firearms are generally not allowed to be used in public, unlike motor vehicles, which are allowed to be used extensively in public, is ignored by the

---

[282] *See* press release of California Assemblymember Phil Ting, Assemblymembers Ting and Gomez Introduce Gun Liability Insurance Bill (Feb. 5, 2013), available at http://asmdc.org/members/a19/news-room/press-releases/assemblymembers-ting-and-gomez-introduce-gun-liability-insurance-bill (Assemblymember Ting stating that [t]he government requires insurance as a condition of operating a car – at the very least we should impose a similar requirement for owning a firearm").

proponents of this measure.

Using the logic of the Sunnyvale Court regarding the fact that "large capacity magazines" represent only a subset of all magazines available for use, or using the San Francisco Court's logic that the availability of local police obviated the need for private ownership of "large capacity magazines", California could ban all private ownership of motor vehicles and argue that public transit and non-motorized vehicles, such as bicycles and skateboards, are reasonable substitutes.

It's not just homosexual sexual activity and cars that could be banned. To combat obesity, which accounts for far more deaths than firearms-related homicides, food of all types, from candy to fast food to bacon to just about every other popular food product that is tied to obesity, would be unavailable for purchase or consumption (and there would be strict regulation of the production of such food products in private) and criminal sentences would apply to anyone in possession of those food products.[283]

Since none of driving motor vehicles, eating harmful foods or engaging in homosexual sexual activity is an enumerated constitutional right, if we follow the standards set by the District Court Orders (which used an intermediate scrutiny review for an enumerated constitutional right, a much higher standard than would apply to the foregoing prohibitions/bans) all of the aforementioned regulations would survive constitutional scrutiny.

Returning to the Magazine Bans, let us assume the

---

[283] The prospect of police confiscating donuts is only one terrifying eventuality of such regulation. Though this is obviously tongue-in-cheek, the District Court Orders force us to contemplate the entire range of bans that could be imposed on every day activities.

accuracy of the District Courts' claims that it is rare for any person using a firearm for self defense to fire more than 10 rounds. What, then, about the actual frequency with which mass shootings take place or where "large capacity magazines" are used in a homicide? As this paper has shown, the chance of a fatality occurring from a mass shooting taking place in San Francisco is .000000016% in any year. By comparison, the odds of being struck by lightning in the United States any particular year are 1 in 1,000,000, or .00010%[284] and there were more deaths from lightning strikes in 2011 (39)[285] than from mass shootings

---

[284] *"Lightning: Frequently Asked Questions"*, NATIONAL WEATHER SERVICE website (retrieved April 11, 2014), available at http://www.srh.noaa.gov/jetstream/lightning/lightning_faq.htm.

[285] Id. The total number of deaths from lightning strikes in the US between 2006 and 2012 was 238, an average of 34 per year. *See* John S. Jensenius, Jr., *A Detailed Analysis of Recent Lightning Deaths in the United States*, NATIONAL WEATHER SERVICE study, available at http://www.lightningsafety.noaa.gov/resources/RecentLightningDeaths.pdf.

in an average year (18).[286]

Are we to believe that there is such urgency in preventing an event less likely to occur than a death from lightning strike such that it serves as justification for infringing upon an enumerated constitutional right? Put another way, would any rational person accept a government decree forbidding all outdoors activity premised upon the need to protect against deaths from lightning strikes? By banning lawfully owned and used "large capacity magazines" the cities of San Francisco and Sunnyvale are doing just that.

The City of San Francisco certainly didn't take such draconian action in response to the AIDS epidemic, the source of at least 19,000 fatalities in the city, nor did the State of California, which has seen over 95,000 fatalities

---

[286] *CRS Report*, supra note 40.

from AIDS.

It is not enough to say, as the San Francisco Court did, that citizens should rely upon the police for their self defense needs. The United States Supreme Court has held that citizens do not have an enforceable interest in police protection.[287] For a court to deprive the citizenry of an

---

[287] Castle Rock v. Gonzales, 545 U.S. 748 (2005). *See, also*, DeShaney v. Winnebago County Dept. of Social Services, 489 U.S. 189, 195 (1989) (holding that there is no constitutional requirement of any "[s]tate to protect the life, liberty, and property of its citizens against invasion by private actors") and L. Cary Unkelbach, *No Duty to Protect: Two Exceptions* THE POLICE CHIEF, vol. 71, no. 7 (July 2004),(this publication is the "official publication of the International Association of Chiefs of Police") available at http://www.policechiefmagazine.org/magazine/index.cfm?fuseaction=display_arch&article_id=341&issue_id=72004 : ("Law enforcement generally does not have a federal constitutional duty to protect one private person from another.") It should also be noted that there is no justification for law enforcement being allowed to possess arms that are generally not available to citizens. The Constitution clearly sets out the role of the federal government and the states with regard to the military (including the militia). It is the military, not law enforcement,

enumerated right to self defense based on the assertion that they should rely upon the protection provided by the government, which the government has explicitly disclaimed any obligation to provide, is nothing short of ludicrous. Even if the government did have an obligation to provide for the self defense needs of individual citizens, there is no precedent for the proposition that the government has a monopoly on the provision of such services. In fact, the Second Amendment clearly vests that

---

that has the obligation to defend the country from attack and to prosecute warfare. Law enforcement is a domestic matter and if civilians may not lawfully possess a certain type of arm, there is no reason for law enforcement to possess such an arm. If there is a need for a more heavily armed force, that force is the military, whose weapons are meant to confront similarly equipped opposing forces, not civilians. *See, e.g.,* Randy Balko, *Overkill: The Rise of Paramilitary Police Raids in America* 13 (Cato Institute 2006), available at http://object.cato.org/sites/cato.org/files/pubs/pdf/balko_whitepaper_2006.pdf ("Patrol officers in Indianapolis are now armed with M-16 rifles supplied by the military… Several Chicago-area police departments use the M-16 as well.")

right with the individual.²⁸⁸

Moreover, there may be times, albeit rare, when the individual citizen will not be able look to the government for protection even if the government were otherwise willing to provide the services. This may be the case in a natural disaster, where government services of all types, including police, may be suspended for days or longer, or it could take the form of a fundamental collapse of the rule of law in either a local or national setting.²⁸⁹ If law

---

²⁸⁸ *Heller*, slip op. at 63.

²⁸⁹ The rise of the National Socialist German Workers' Party in the 1930s is an example of this. The Nazi regime first disarmed its victims through the imposition of firearms possession bans on, *inter alia*, Jews, which then enabled the regime to persecute its victims and ultimately slaughter millions of them. *See generally,* STEPHEN P. HALBROOK, GUN CONTROL IN THE THIRD REICH: DISARMING JEWS AND "ENEMIES OF THE STATE" (2014). The author of this paper is the son of a Holocaust survivor. The bulk of his mother's family, other than her mother and father, were killed by the Nazis in the Czech Republic (at the time, Czechoslovakia). Because the author's maternal grandfather's father was a naturalized United States citizen, the author's maternal

grandfather was treated as an American by the Nazi regime, notwithstanding the fact that the family was Jewish and he had never been to the United States to claim citizenship. Nonetheless, through the auspices of the International Red Cross, the author's maternal grandfather was allowed to travel to the United States to claim citizenship. During that period, however, the Nazi SS abducted the author's maternal grandmother and his mother. Only when the United States arranged for a swap of German captives for Americans being held overseas (which the author's mother and maternal grandmother qualified for upon his maternal grandfather claiming United States citizenship) did the Nazis release the author's mother and maternal grandmother. Many of the remaining members of the family were slaughtered in the Theresienstadt death camp. *See, e.g.,* Holocaust database entry at Yad Vashem prepared by the author's maternal grandmother, available at http://db.yadvashem.org/names/nameDetails.html?itemId=934838&language=en#!prettyPhoto. The point of this personal anecdote is to show that while many people consider events such as the Holocaust to be apocryphal or incapable of being repeated, such events occur with relative frequency in history and in the western world. *See, e.g.,* PAUL MOJZES BALKAN GENOCIDES: HOLOCAUST AND ETHNIC CLEANSING IN THE TWENTIETH CENTURY (Rowman & Littlefield 2011) for a study of three separate occurrences of genocide in the Balkan peninsula during the 20th century. Furthermore, at the time of the writing of this paper, a state of near-civil war exists in Ukraine. Not only are citizens of Ukraine without effective police or military protection from Russian provocateurs, there have been reports of militants targeting Jews for

enforcement is exempt from the restrictions of anti-gun laws such as the Magazine Bans, it can only be because they are allowed to protect themselves against the rare threat posed by assailants who either outnumber law enforcement or are armed with illegal weapons having greater firepower than the law-abiding citizen has. As it happens, the average number of shots fired by police in a

---

"registration" leading to deportation or forfeiture of citizenship, or worse. *See,* Michael Margalit, *Donetsk leaflet: Jews must register or face deportation*, YNETNEWS.COM (April 16, 2014), available at http://www.ynetnews.com/articles/0,7340,L-4510688,00.html ("A leaflet distributed in Donetsk, Ukraine calling for all Jews over 16 years old to register as Jews marred the Jewish community's Passover festivities Monday (Passover eve), replacing them with feelings of concern. The leaflet demanded the city's Jews supply a detailed list of all the property they own, or else have their citizenship revoked, face deportation and see their assets confiscated.") While it is unclear whether the leaflets were distributed by any governmental authority or even whether they were anything more than factional agitprop, they point to a long history of minority groups being persecuted by larger, more powerful groups of individuals or governments.

typical incident is well under 10 rounds.[290]

In fact, in the 2011 report on New York Police Department Firearms Discharges, the most frequent number of rounds fired by a New York Police Department officer was one,[291] which is clearly below the average of 2.1-2.2 rounds fired by citizens in self defense situations, as found by the District Courts.

Rare as the need for more than 10 rounds may be, the Constitution is a document that protects the rights of citizens not only in ordinary times but, in particular, extraordinary times. As the data on the average number of rounds fired by law enforcement show, it is no less

---

[290] Al Baker, *11 Years of Police Gunfire, in Painstaking Detail*, N.Y. TIMES (May 8, 2008), available at http://www.nytimes.com/2008/05/08/nyregion/08nypd.html?pagewanted=all.

[291] *See supra* note 63.

extraordinary for a citizen to need the right to choose an arm that is useful in self defense, such as a "large capacity magazine", than it is for a law enforcement officer to need such right. Once a right, such as the right to bear arms for self defense, and in particular, a specific type of arm like a "large capacity magazine", is extinguished (or worse, reserved for the quasi-noble political class), its benefits can't easily be returned to the people in a time of need. If there comes a time when a "large capacity magazine" is the difference between a citizens life and death, what then of the District Courts' pronouncement that the rarity of the situation warranted the destruction of the right?

vi) Proposed Standard for Second Amendment Cases

While this paper has shown that "large capacity magazines" do not present an unreasonable risk to public safety (either in the absolute number of fatalities that can be attributed to them or the number of fatalities relative to other modalities, such as AIDS or motor vehicles), there is obviously a place for reasonable regulations of arms under the Second Amendment.

What is not tolerable is an outright ban on any class of arms, as there is no precedent in relevant jurisprudence for such a draconian and overbroad approach. In *Heller*, Justice Scalia provided the needed guidance for how to examine Second Amendment cases: base the review on the same principles as would apply to First Amendment cases.

As such, whether the standard of review is intermediate scrutiny or strict scrutiny, the methodology for court inquiry should have the same starting point: the government satisfying its burden of proof that the arm is the cause of a definable problem in need of solving. To do this, it is not enough to simply present horrific, yet isolated, incidents of arms abuse. The particular arm has to be examined to determine the scope of lawful uses of the arm, which can then be compared to the incidences of unlawful uses, in order to balance the rights of law abiding citizens against the need for public safety. A form of this was done in *Brown*, *Morales,* the Stop and Frisk Cases and *Schenck*. In each case, fears of horrific, yet relatively isolated, consequences of the exercise of a right did not support the mass and absolute infringement of an entire constituency's individual rights.

When it comes to absolute bans on a class of arms, the *Heller* court was absolutely clear of such a review: "Under any of the standards of scrutiny that we have applied to enumerated constitutional rights, banning from the home 'the most preferred firearm in the nation to 'keep' and use for protection of one's home and family,' would fail constitutional muster"²⁹² and " ... the enshrinement of constitutional rights necessarily takes certain policy choices off the table. These include the absolute prohibition of handguns held and used for self-defense in the home."²⁹³

The *Heller* court went on to deal with the same "subset" argument made by the Sunnyvale Court and found "[i]t is no answer to say, as petitioners do, that it is permissible to ban the possession of handguns so long as the possession of other firearms (i.e., long guns) is allowed...a complete prohibition of their use is invalid."²⁹⁴ Likewise, it is no answer to say that it is permissible to ban the possession of "large capacity magazines" because the possession of other magazines is allowed.

Even if using the lower standard of intermediate

---

²⁹² *Heller*, slip op. at 56-57.

²⁹³ Id. at 64.

²⁹⁴ *Id*. at 57-58.

scrutiny, which may be appropriate for laws that do not effect a absolute ban on arms, the threshold set forth in *Turner* has to be met. That is, courts must review the government's justifications for regulation to "…assure that, in formulating its judgments, [government] has drawn reasonable inferences based on substantial evidence…."[295] This was not done by the District Courts; instead, they rubberstamped the government's conclusions and ignored the evidence presented by the laws' challengers. The Sunnyvale Court claimed that it was not its place to determine the exact effect of the Sunnyvale Magazine Ban; rather, it was charged with concentrating on "…the relationship between the challenged ordinance and public safety…."[296] By giving nothing more than a facial examination to Sunnyvale's claims regarding the actual threat posed by "large capacity magazine", the Sunnyvale

---

[295] *See supra* note 109 and accompanying text.

[296] Sunnyvale Order, *supra* note 2, at 13.

Court failed to require the government to establish its burden of proof, under *Turner* and any other recognized standard of intermediate scrutiny review.

Indeed, there is in fact a way for Sunnyvale and San Francisco to further the goals of protecting public safety: Just as in *McCullen*[297], the government has an obligation to

---

[297] *Supra* note 90. In *McCullen*, the Supreme Court pointed out that the state's justification for doubling the size of a no-speech zone outside of an abortion clinic was not sufficient to warrant the effect of the law, which was to block an important means of communication for pro-life individuals. In that case, the state claimed that it was too difficult to enforce the existing law because it was difficult to pick out violators and a larger zone would facilitate enforcement. The Supreme Court, however, stated that while the enlarged zone might facilitate enforcement, it would also negatively impact the ability of pro-life individuals to communicate with patients and the state had an obligation to make a greater effort at enforcing the existing zone. In many ways this is directly analogous to firearms bans, including the Magazine Bans. To wit, rather than infringe the rights of all firearms owners in an attempt to prevent the rare mass shooting, the state should devote greater resources to prosecuting violations of existing law that was enacted to eliminate violence.

enforce existing laws that further the goal of public safety before they engage in the extraordinary act of a blanket infringement of an enumerated constitutional right.

In truth, laws that ban an entire class of arms, as the Magazine Bans do, are invalid on their face. The *Heller* court considered and rejected Justice Breyer's proposal that Second Amendment cases be judged under an "interest-balancing approach", where the law's burden is balanced against the government interests involved.[298] Interest-balancing is what the District Courts did in reviewing the Magazine Bans, and what Justice Scalia said in *Heller* should apply to the District Court Orders:

> We know of no other enumerated constitutional right whose core protection has been subjected to a freestanding "interest-balancing"

---

[298] *Heller*, slip op. at 62.

approach. The very enumeration of the right takes out of the hands of government—even the Third Branch of Government—the power to decide on a case-by-case basis whether the right is really worth insisting upon. A constitutional guarantee subject to future judges' assessments of its usefulness is no constitutional guarantee at all…We would not apply an "interest-balancing" approach to the prohibition of a peaceful neo-Nazi march through Skokie. *See National Socialist Party of America v. Skokie*, 432 U. S. 43 (1977) (*per curiam*). The First Amendment contains the freedom-of-speech guarantee that the people ratified, which included exceptions for obscenity, libel, and disclosure of state secrets, but not for the expression of extremely unpopular and wrong-headed views. The Second Amendment is no different. Like the First, it is the very product of an interest-balancing by the people—which Justice

Breyer would now conduct for them anew. And whatever else it leaves to future evaluation, it surely elevates above all other interests the right of law-abiding, responsible citizens to use arms in defense of hearth and home.[299]

So a city could arguably restrict the possession of "large capacity magazines" to the home or for use when hunting, if it could satisfy the requisite burden of proof, and it could ban completely the possession of arms that are not subject to the protections of the Second Amendment (such as the fully automatic-capable military M-16 rifle, as Justice Scalia acknowledged in *Heller*[300]). But just as *Heller* noted that a peaceful neo-Nazi march would be protected absolutely by the First Amendment, the core protections of the Second Amendment-the right to arms

---

[299] *Id.* at 63.

[300] *Id.* at 55.

commonly possessed and lawfully used for self defense and hunting, such as "large capacity magazines"-are not subject to the type of interest balancing that the District Courts engaged in. Collective punishment of the entire law-abiding population for the misdeeds of criminals simply has no precedent or justification under the Constitution.

In deferring to the government over protected individual rights, the Sunnyvale Court quoted the text from *Heller* above, yet in quoting it, failed to properly understand its meaning.[301] If "[a] constitutional guarantee subject to future judges' assessments of its usefulness is no constitutional guarantee at all" then one subject to the whim of a few voters or legislators is even less of a constitutional guarantee. The quoted text means that neither the judiciary nor the legislature nor even a mere majority of

---

[301] *Sunnyvale Order, supra* note 2, at 13. (quoting from *Helller* "A constitutional guarantee subject to future judges' assessments of its usefulness is no constitutional guarantee at all. ")

voters in a single election with a sparse voter turnout have the power to strip from the people the rights guaranteed by the Second Amendment. Yet, in rubberstamping the acts of Sunnyvale and San Francisco to deprive a minority group of its enumerated Second Amendment rights, the District Courts did exactly that which the *Heller* court sought to prohibit.

Even if, somehow, it were to be determined that "large capacity magazines" are not at the core of the Second Amendment, and thus susceptible to an interest-balancing type of review, at the very least, the causation threshold Justice Scalia employed in *Brown* is the only reasonable and justifiable standard to use. It is no coincidence that Justice Scalia, who wrote the *Brown* opinion (a First Amendment case), also wrote the *Heller* opinion and pointed to First Amendment standards for Second Amendment Cases. Government has a heavy burden when it seeks to infringe enumerated, constitutional rights; causation, not correlation, is the threshold to be met, and isolated incidents of abuse of a right do not establish causation.

vii) Conclusion

In the face of a federal government that has morphed from one of limited, enumerated rights into an omnipotent force that increasingly acts as though it is the source of, and arbiter of, individual rights, the District Court Orders remind us of the risks of ignoring the rule of law and the power of reason.

This paper has illustrated the consequences of lawmaking that is premised on preventing horrible, yet exceedingly rare, abuses of constitutional rights. Pointing to a tragedy like the massacres at Sandy Hook or

Columbine can certainly lead to a populist cry for action but it neither satisfies the legal requirements for infringing enumerated constitutional rights nor comports with the significant interest the judicial branch (and society at large) has in protecting the rights of minority constituencies. Just as federal courts in *Perry* defended a minority from what it saw to be an irrational and hate based attack on an unenumerated and unacknowledged right, courts should not be cowed into upholding infringements on the enumerated Second Amendment right to arms by fear mongering groups using sensationalistic, irrelevant data .

It should be noted that one of the legislative findings in the San Francisco Magazine Ban was a desire to prevent a reoccurrence of the Sandy Hook massacre. The violent video game ban championed by disgraced Senator Yee in *Brown* was based on a similar finding. Because no stronger case can be made that "large capacity magazines" cause massacres than was made to show that violent video games cause massacres, the precedent set in *Brown* for overturning AB1179 should result in the overturning of the Magazine Bans.

Furthermore, if "large capacity magazines" can be banned on the basis of protecting public safety, a stronger empirical case can be made for banning everything from motor vehicles to Craigslist personal ads. While this paper has used the Magazine Bans as a focal point, the arguments presented herein would apply with equal force to bans on "assault weapons" or any other class of arms in common, lawful use.

At the time of the publication of this paper, two tragic events occurred in southern California that put a point on the themes explored herein. On May 21, 2014, four people were killed and 20 injured when a passenger bus and a semi-tractor truck collided outside of Blythe, California.³⁰² Other than a few perfunctory wire service stories, very little media attention was paid to this incident and its fatalities. Two days later, also in southern California, a deranged assailant shot and killed three people in Isla Vista, California.³⁰³ Unlike the four deaths from the vehicle accident two days prior, the Isla Vista shooting received round-the-clock news coverage³⁰⁴ and was used

---

³⁰² http://articles.chicagotribune.com/2014-05-21/news/sns-rt-us-usa-buscrash-california-20140521_1_california-highway-patrol-passenger-bus-bus-driver

³⁰³ Kate Mather, Matt Stevens, *UCSB sorority targeted by Isla Vista shooting suspect urges privacy*. L.A. TIMES (May 25, 2014), available at http://www.latimes.com/local/lanow/la-me-ln-sorority-isla-vista-privacy-20140525-story.html. In addition to shooting and killing three people, the assailant stabbed and killed three other people and used his car as a weapon to injure numerous other victims before he took his own life. *Id.* Because this incident is being discussed in the context of firearms laws and public safety claims, the focus herein will be solely on the shooting victims.

³⁰⁴ A Google search performed on May 27, 2014 using the search term "UCSB shooting" returned over 1 million results. On the same date, a Google search using the terms "El Paso-Los Angeles Limousine

by political figures to renew calls for new, draconian firearms laws.[305]

It is important to note that the assailant in the Isla Vista shootings complied with California law in purchasing the firearms he used, including existing law prohibiting the purchase of "large capacity magazines".[306] Clearly, the

---

Express" "Blythe" (the name of the bus involved in the accident and the location of the accident) returned only 492 results. Screen prints of the searches and results are on file with the author.

[305] *Liberal senator says gun-control laws proposed after Newtown massacre could have prevented UCSB shootings, but ordinary Americans aren't sure,* DAILY MAIL ONLINE (May 26, 2014), available at http://www.dailymail.co.uk/news/article-2639888/Liberal-senator-says-gun-control-laws-proposed-Newtown-massacre-prevented-UCSB-shootings-ordinary-Americans-arent-sure.html.

[306] *Id.* ("The handguns guns and ammunition found near Rodger's body on Friday night were all purchased legally.") Though the police report on this incident has not been published at the time of the publication of this paper, all available information indicates that the assailant used three handguns that were lawfully purchased in California within the last year or so. Since "large capacity magazines" were not legal for purchase in California at all relevant times, it appears that the

public safety justifications upon which the District Court Orders were based did not prevent the Isla Vista shootings. In point of fact, the assailant in the Isla Vista shootings was, like the assailant in the Sandy Hook massacre, a mentally ill person obsessed with violent video games and other media.[307] In particular, both assailants were addicted

---

assailant used three handguns, each with no more than a 10 round magazine. The San Francisco Order, at 7, endorsed the idea that a person interested in firing more than 10 rounds could simply use more than 1 of the lawful 10 round magazines (and, presumably, more than 1 firearm), only this endorsement was as an explanation for why the San Francisco Magazine Ban did not destroy the right to self-defense. Indeed, what the Isla Vista shooting shows is that magazine limitations and other draconian firearms restrictions won't impede the destruction of a determined assailant. The only thing such limitations and restrictions do is infringe upon the enumerated Constitutional rights of law-abiding citizens.

[307] In a 141 page manifesto published shortly before he began his attacks, Elliot Rodger, the assailant in the Isla Vista shootings, described a lifetime of playing various violent video games, including "World of Warcraft" as well as his lengthy battle with mental illness. See Linda Massarella, Sophia Rosenbaum and Leonard Greene, *The Vile Manifesto of a Killer*, N.Y. POST (May 25, 2014) (containing a link to

to the "World of Warcraft" video game.[308]

Not only did California's extreme firearms laws fail to prevent the Isla Vista shootings, the utter lack of media and political attention devoted to other fatal incidents, like the four fatalities in the Blythe bus incident two days prior to the Isla Vista shootings negatively skew the public's view of the actual risks posed by firearms and effectively whitewashes the far greater risks that exist on an everyday basis.

Indeed, as if on cue, California's reliably knee-jerk legislature did not waste time in turning the Isla Vista murders into a means to further its obsession with attacking Second Amendment rights. Ignoring the fact that three of the murders were committed with knives and many of those

---

the full text of the assailant's manifesto, a copy of which is on file with the author).

[308] *Id.* and The Lanza Report, *supra* note 15.

injured were harmed by the assailant's automobile, California Democrats introduced a bill in the State Assembly ("AB 1014") to create a mechanism whereby law enforcement could confiscate firearms (but not knives or automobiles or any other deadly weapons) from individuals who have been accused of presenting ambiguous risks of violence.[309]

Under proposed AB 1014, pursuant to an ex parte proceeding where a magistrate is presented with a statement from any individual that such individual believes another individual "...poses a significant risk of personal injury to himself or herself or others by possessing

---

[309] CAL. ASSEMBLY BILL 1014 (2013-2014 Session) *An act to amend Section 18250 of, and to add Division 3.2 (commencing with Section 18100) to Title 2 of Part 6 of, the Penal Code, and to amend Section 8105 of the Welfare and Institutions Code, relating to firearms* (version dated 5/28/14, on file with the author), available at http://leginfo.legislature.ca.gov/faces/billNavClient.xhtml?bill_id=201320140AB1014#.

firearms…"[310], the magistrate can, without any further proceedings, order law enforcement to confiscate all firearms possessed by the subject of the order. Knives, vehicles and all other deadly weapons would be outside the scope of the order, and for a period of two weeks the subject of the order will not even have the opportunity to challenge the order.[311] Stripped of due process rights, humiliated by anonymous accusations and the whim of a magistrate who likely would prefer to err on the side of caution, the subject of the AB 1014 order would be presumed guilty of a prospective violent crime and have his or her enumerated, constitutional right to possess a firearm for self defense terminated until the court proceeding weeks down the line, where he or she will have to endure a Kafkaesque hearing to reclaim his or her basic rights.[312]

---

[310] *Id.*

[311] *Id.*

[312] The topic of due process rights and proposed AB 1014 is the subject of an upcoming paper from the author.

Imagine if a person accused of having AIDS and engaging in unsafe sex with unwitting partners were subject to a similar order prohibiting him or her from engaging in any sexual acts until a court determined that there was no such risk. It is no exaggeration to presume that civil unrest would quickly spread throughout urban areas of California.

The precedent being set by lower courts, such as in the District Court Orders, may be one that liberal activists applaud today, but it is also one that will certainly be used to attack rights, including unenumerated rights such as abortion, same sex marriage and homosexual sexual activity, that have far less robust constitutional protections than the Second Amendment provides.

If an entire class of arms, protected by the Second Amendment, that is responsible for at most an estimated

228 fatalities in California can be banned as a threat to public safety, how could homosexual sexual activity, which isn't an enumerated constitutional right and is responsible for approximately five times the number of casualties as "large capacity magazines", be protected?

Far from being a call for banning homosexual sexual activity or the use of motor vehicles, this paper is a call for the return of the primacy of individual rights. Only if courts are held to a standard of (i) absolutely protecting core enumerated rights and (ii) placing on the government the burden of proving that the exercise of non-core rights is the principal *cause* of (not just correlated with) a significant societal problem, where the magnitude of the problem conclusively outweighs the right to lawful exercise of such right and narrowly drawn regulation is the only workable and reasonable solution thereto, will minority rights be protected.

Indeed, while this paper has focused on the Magazine Bans, the underlying risks of infringing any other aspect of the rights protected by the Second Amendment based upon an appeal to public safety apply equally. Whether it's a ban on magazines, a ban on "assault weapons" or an ex parte suspension of the basic right to own a firearm for self defense, as would be the case if AB 1014 were enacted in California, any infringement of rights clocked in the guise of a need for public safety should be seen as suspect.

After noting the same dichotomy between the treatment of unenumerated gay rights and enumerated firearms rights as this paper has elaborated upon, Professor Glenn Reynolds famously said "[p]ersonally, I'd be delighted to live in a country where happily married gay couples had closets full of assault weapons."[313]

I happen to agree entirely with Professor Reynolds, but, as this paper has demonstrated, if the precedent of the Magazine Bans is set, courts will have no impediment to inverting our legal system of rights protection, creating a presumption that government has the right to infringe upon even the most basic of rights unless the aggrieved citizen can accomplish the Sisyphean task of proving that the need for that right outweighs the government's desire to infringe upon it.

Under such a system, rights assumed to exist, enumerated or not, longstanding and newly formed alike, including the rights to same sex marriage and same sex sexual activity, will be supplanted by a government that

---

[313] *Gays and Guns,* posted on INSTAPUNDIT.COM (Oct. 4, 2004), available at http://pjmedia.com/instapundit/48538/.

metes out and denies rights on whim, or worse.